Men Who Loved

Men Who Loved

Brad Barham

Bridgeview Press
Philadelphia

Table of Contents

Being deeply loved by someone gives you strength, while loving someone deeply gives you courage.

Lao Tzu

Chapter 1

The siren grew louder and then whined down as the ambulance exited I-95. The red and white emergency vehicle screeched to a halt beside the crumpled car, which blocked the end of the off ramp. The ambulance emptied three EMTs.

Unsteady and slightly confused, Jack stood by his wrecked car, holding his hand over a bleeding gash on his head. "I'm okay," he said to an EMT. "Take care of Ken. He doesn't look too good. I think he's unconscious."

Moments later, a state police car, light bar flashing and siren screaming, stopped behind the ambulance. A trooper jumped out yelling, "How's everybody?"

Looking up from the patient just placed on a trauma board, an EMT said, "Think we have everything under control but better block off this ramp or we'll all be in trouble."

The trooper ran back to his car and parked it perpendicular to the ramp entrance, blocking possible exiting traffic.

Minutes later, the ambulance turned around and headed up the ramp.

The trooper backed his car onto the shoulder of the interstate then exited the vehicle and waved traffic to the left lanes. This allowed the ambulance to reenter the highway. It then sped away, carrying Jack and Ken to the hospital.

While sirens howled, an EMT placed an oxygen mask over Ken's mouth and nose as another man started an IV. The first EMT started an electrocardio-gram and monitored Ken's heartbeat. The other EMT repeatedly took Ken's blood pressure.

With on-board telemetry, the electrocardiogram and blood pressure readings were sent to a doctor awaiting the patient's arrival at the emergency room.

"You okay?" an EMT asked Jack who visibly shook while holding his bandaged head and stared at Ken who lay motionless on the stretcher.

"How could this happen?" Jack asked. *Please, God, don't let him die. I need him. Please don't let him die.*

Holding Ken's hand, Jack attempted to mentally suppress the sound of the siren as he recalled the wonderful things the couple had shared over the past fifty years. His fondest memory was their wedding. He squeezed Ken's hand and mentally replayed the event.

The scent of incense and smoke competed with the echoes of holy words and sacred music for space in the gothic-style Greenwich Village Episcopal church.

"I now pronounce you legally married," Father Mulhony said to Jack, "You may now kiss your spouse."

Jack, a tall handsome man of seventy, had deep-blue eyes. He grinned and stared at Ken, seventy-two.

Despite a few tears, Ken's brown eyes sparkled as he grinned back. They kissed, and then the gray haired men hugged as the congregation clapped their approval.

The organist floored the organ's volume pedal, filling the church with the floor shaking sounds of Handel's *The Arrival of the Queen of Sheba* to mark the end of the ceremony. The smiling couple waved to the congregation from the altar while friends clicked away with cell phones and cameras.

Photos completed, the grinning couple strolled down the aisle, shaking hands and exchanging greetings with guests.

"Can you believe it?" Jack asked, squeezing Ken's hand.

"It's been a long time coming," Ken said, beaming with pride.

"More like a lifetime, I'd say."

"Several life times but we did it."

The wedding party walked outside the church where a commercial photographer, George, took photographs as passersby on the sidewalk stopped to watch the festivities.

A boy, tugging at his mother's arm, was heard to say, "Look momma. Those men are kissing."

"I'm guessing they've just been married," the woman said. "Those are *gay* men."

"They do look happy don't they?" the boy asked.

The mother laughed. "Yes, they're *happy*."

Laughing, Jack turned to Ken, "Did you hear that kid?"

"Yes. We are *happy*."

George took the last photo then scanned the camera screen to confirm the quality of the picture then said, "Well, guys. That's it for now. Let's get on with the rest of your life."

Ken turned and called to his friends. "Everyone. Join us in the church hall for a long overdue celebration."

Harry, a friend of the couple for twenty-five years shouted, "Yeah. Let's get the drinking started. Where's the bar?"

"I'm all for that," George yelled. "Ken, you and

Jack go on in."

The officiating priest, still wearing his rainbow colored stole, waited for the couple and guests in the church social hall. The caterers fussed with candles and adjusted floral arrangements placed around the room. As the couple entered the hall, the priest and caterers clapped and roared their approval.

The caterer / wedding planner, Maurice, an African-American friend of the couple, took Ken and Jack by the arm. "You two stand by the registration table. Father, would you stand beside Jack?"

Maurice stepped back and said, "That's the finest, honkey reception line I've ever seen."

Maurice ran his hand over his straightened, shiny-black hair, smoothed his white tuxedo, adjusted his red bow tie, and then opened the social hall doors. Please," he said to the waiting guests, "Come in and meet the happy new couple."

Harry was first in line. He shook hands with the priest. "Father, thank you for making these guys legal."

Ken rubbed his plump belly and chuckled, "Just in time for the baby to have his father's last name."

The priest looked at Harry, laughed, and then said, "I've agreed to baptize it as soon as it's born."

One hundred and seven guests signed the registry and then did their best to empty the bar. Among the guests were: Ken's boyhood friend Tim; Ken' brother, Leonard and his wife, Martha; Jack's sister, Linda, and her twenty-one year old son, William, who flew in the morning of the wedding.

Leonard and Martha gave the couple a group-hug. "We're so happy for you guys."

Ken grinned. "Now, we're equal to you heteros."

Linda first hugged Jack and kissed him on the cheek. "Congratulations, honey. My little brother has finally done it." She kissed Ken and said, "Take good care of my brother."

"I will," Ken said and smiled. "I promise."

"For all these years, you've done a good job," Linda said. "Don't stop."

William was next to greet the couple. He gave the two men a group hug and kissed each on the cheek. "Uncle Jack. Uncle Ken. I'm so happy for you guys. I hadn't told you before, but there's a chance you might be attending another wedding in a few months."

The couple stood back and looked at William in disbelief.

"Are you marrying Janet?" Jack asked.

"I am. We're planning the wedding now. I think it'll be in November. All depends on the availability of a certain hall she insists on using."

Jack kissed his nephew on the cheek, hugged him and smiled. "I'm so happy for you. Janet is a wonderful girl. I wouldn't mind if she made me a great uncle."

"Let's not get too far ahead," William chuckled.

Ken hugged William. "You and Janet will make a wonderful couple. Don't forget to send us an invitation."

The couple took their seats at the head table where they could see the buffet line and had access to the dance floor.

The DJ had been playing quiet reception music, but a cue from Maurice had the DJ play a recorded drum roll.

Leonard, carrying a microphone, walked to the middle of the gothic hall once a church sanctuary. "Father, ladies, gentlemen, and *others*," he said,

13

stifling a chuckle. "I propose a toast to Ken, my friend and adopted baby brother, and Jack, my new brother-in-law. May they have a wonderful married life and relationship which lasts another fifty years."

The guests raised their glasses in a toast. "To the couple." They then filled the hall with shouting and clapping. The three British guests yelled, "Here. Here."

"Next," Leonard said, his voice booming from big-box speakers, "I would like to introduce Father Mulhoney."

The priest walked to the middle of the floor and took the mike. "Thank you, Leonard. This is a memorable day for lots of people." Gesturing toward the newly married couple, he continued. "First, for Jack and Ken. After living together fifty years, without benefit of clergy, they are now legally married."

The crowd broke out in boisterous applause. One chubby man continued to clap vigorously long after everyone else had stopped.

The priest nodded to the clapping man then said, "Thank you, sir. We have New York's legislature and governor to thank for this occasion. This is the first legal gay marriage ceremony I have had the pleasure of conducting. This is the first gay marriage ceremony in this church. This is also the first gay wedding reception held in this hall, and Ken said something about being the first gay man to have a baby."

The crowd laughed so loudly the DJ put in his ear plugs.

Ken stood and rubbed his plump belly. "The baby has been in here for forty-nine years, waiting for the day he could have legal parents and a proper surname. Now it can come out—oops—I meant it could be delivered."

Maurice laughed and then shouted, "Don't worry. If labor starts during the party, we have clean tablecloths, string, and scissors, and it doesn't take long to boil water. Oh, I forgot to say we also have a doctor in the house."

Someone at the back table shouted, "Yeah. A psychiatrist."

Jack hugged Ken and laughed. "I've waited this long, Bud. I can wait until you get to the hospital for the delivery."

The DJ played 60's and 70's dance music.

Many of the guests walked or limped to the dance floor. Arthritis, artificial knees and hips, lubricated by ample amounts of champagne, didn't hinder the guest's reliving their disco days even if their steps were slow, off beat, and sometimes painful. For a short time, it seemed everyone believed they were twenty again.

Jack and Ken chose to have a buffet instead of a sit-down dinner. As the caterer began uncovering various hot foods, a few guests lined up to eat.

Winston, who had been sitting out the dancing, rushed to the buffet, pushing his walker. Harold, a longtime friend of Winston was second in line.

Harold turned to Winston and said, "This looks better than the early bird special at Diamond's doesn't it?"

Taking a second piece of prime rib, Winston said, "Nah. I prefer to be served than do this self-service stuff while I'm on my walker."

"Want me to carry that food to your table?" Harold asked.

"Thanks, but I can manage, despite this damn walker."

The food line moved slowly. People who were once strangers had time to start conversations and develop relationships while waiting for chafing dishes to be refilled.

Don, a man of fifty, tapped the shoulder of the man in front of him. "How long have you known Jack and Ken?"

"About thirty years," the stranger replied. "By the way, I'm Eugene. My friends call me Gene."

The men shook hands.

"Nice to meet you, Gene. I'm Don. I've known Jack and Ken since we were deck hands on Noah's ark. We met in the seventies in the South Mountain Park in South Orange in Jersey. The place used to be very "cruisy." In those days, there weren't many gay bars, so guys met in out-of-the-way places—like parks."

"Careful, Don," Jack said. "You don't want to say too much—if you know what I mean."

"Oh, I know all about *that* park and others," Gene said. "I lived in New York and used to cruise Central Park, especially the area known as the rocks."

"What era are you talking about?" Don asked.

"The 70s."

"Surely there were gay bars in the city then."

Gene said, "There were, but I lived near the park, and the closest bar was several blocks away. The rocks were convenient and a twenty-four hours a day cruising spot."

"You hussy," Don said and then smiled as if hiding a secret. "I preferred New York's bath houses."

"Me too. Especially the Everard Baths—sometimes called the ever hard. I liked the steam room with its asp-like architecture. When the steam wasn't too thick, you could appreciate its colorful mosaics. Unfortunately, they contained no nudes—just geo-

16

metrics and flowers."

Don smiled and looked Gene in the eye. "No one went to the Everard to admire the mosaics. The steam prevented that and saved who knows how many people from being seen in the wrong place at the wrong time."

"Yeah. Europe had its iron curtain, and we had Everard's steam curtain."

"Did you ever go to the Continental Baths?" Don asked, picking up a plate and flatware at the beginning of the salad area. "Some people called it Club Vapors."

"You bet I did," Gene bragged. "I went there on weekends. There was always some kind of special entertainment around its pool."

"How well I remember that place?"

Gene rolled his eyes then spooned some vegetables onto his plate. "I remember the maze of black ceramic walls in the steam room and the hooks for hanging your towel just outside the door by the pool. Its coping area was the space where all the entertainment took place. It was weird because there were often straight people and couples sitting by the pool, waiting to see the show. They didn't seem to mind all the naked guys exiting the steam room to dry off." Gene slowly bent over to pick up a dropped fork then continued. "As a matter of fact, I think the women liked seeing those naked guys even if they were gay. Some were built like brick shit houses."

"I remember seeing one of the Whiting sisters perform there. Bette Midler and Barry Manilow sang there and several famous pianists performed there. The good thing about the shows was we got to see future stars perform just for the price of admission to the bath."

"I still have a birthday present from there when

the Vapors was in its heyday."

"What kind of present?"

"A blue beach towel. In twelve-inch-high white embroidered letters was written *Continental Baths*."

"Now that's an antique," Don chuckled. "Maybe it's worth some money among the older gay crowd."

"Would you mind if I joined you while we eat?" Gene asked, putting the last possible morsel of food on his already full plate.

"Please do. There are several guys I think you'd like to meet."

Don and Gene made their way across the dance floor, protecting their plates and champagne from being upset by dancers and food jockeys.

Maurice asked the DJ to play some slow dance music and then pulled Jack and Ken onto the dance floor. The guests stopped their activities to clap and watch the couple dance cheek-to-cheek.

Ken whispered in Jack's ear, "Do you remember fifty years ago?"

"I do," Jack said, smiling.

"Where were we?"

"We were cruising each other in some dirty bar in Greenwich Village."

"My memory isn't what it used to be," Ken said, "but I'll never forget that day, or should I say that night?"

"It had to be after midnight. Nothing got started until then."

"Or later."

Jack paused speaking for a moment. "We went back to my Brooklyn apartment and stayed in bed for three days."

"I'm glad that little grocery store on the corner delivered food, or we would have died from too

18

much sex and starvation."

"No we wouldn't. We would have lived on love or was it lust?"

The men swirled in the middle of the dance floor, half-attempted a dip, and then danced around the edge of the hardwood that defined the dance area. The guests clapped their approval.

Gene and Don paused their trek to their table to watch Ken and Jack dance.

As Don reached his table, he said, "Guys, I want you to meet Gene, a longtime friend of Jack and Ken. He's from the city."

Everyone knew the word *city* meant Manhattan.

Gene shook hands with Francis, a retired English teacher; Robert, an ex-Catholic priest; Bill, a retired Methodist minister; Stanley, an architect; Seymour, a young rabbi; Woody, a retired carpenter; Wren, a plumber; Bruce, a retired florist; and Albert, or Al, a nurse. After the introductions, Don and Gene took seats and started some lively conversations about religion and politics.

"Hey guys," Gene said, "the couple is cutting the wedding cake. Should we indulge?"

"Let's," Robert said, "I want a piece of that upper layer. I like red cream cheese icing."

"I'm going to wait a few minutes," Gene said. "It's going to be a while until they get to the bottom layer with the purple icing. That's my favorite color."

Several guests stood around the dessert table, staring at the six-layer cake. Each layer had the color of a stripe in the rainbow flag.

Jack cut a piece of cake and fed it to Ken. "Don't forget to take extra insulin for all this sugar," Jack said.

Chapter 2

After all the food had been eaten and the booze consumed, the party came to a close and the last guest departed. The couple got into a waiting limousine and returned to the semi-rural New Jersey home they had lived in for thirty years.

Jack fumbled forever in his pockets for the house key. Ken was about to begin a search of his own pockets for his key when Jack said, "Found it." Jack opened the heavy oak door and said, "Permit me."

At first, Ken appeared confused about Jack's intention then realized the reason for Jack's actions.

Jack picked up Ken. "A groom always carries his spouse across the threshold the first time they enter their home as a married couple."

Inside, Ken kissed Jack on the cheek, and then the men made their way to the bedroom.

With the aid of Viagra, the men enjoyed their honeymoon.

Chapter 3

Two years later

"Get up," Ken said, shaking Jack's shoulder. "Wake up. You have a doctor appointment in ninety minutes."

"Keep your drawers on," Jack mumbled, tugging at the sheets. "I need another five minutes."

"Remember, you pay for the appointment if you fail to show up without cancelling—*in advance*."

Jack forced himself from bed, coughed several times then slowly made his way to the bathroom.

With great concern, Ken watched his slow-moving lover and prayed, *God, don't let them find anything bad.*

Jack finally finished dressing and sat on the bed.

"What's wrong?" Ken asked.

Jack took a deep breath, gripped the bedspread with both hands and stared at his lover. "I'm feeling awful. Tired."

"Did you cough up any more blood?"

"A few flecks," Jack said, shaking his head.

"Want me to drive?"

"Would you mind?"

"Of course not," Ken replied. "Rest there a minute and I'll get the car cooled off. Be right back."

Ken took a few deep breaths, closed his eyes, and told himself, *Something's not right.*

He returned and helped Jack down the steps and into the cooled Volvo.

Jack had the last appointment of the morning and found the doctor's waiting room empty.

"Jack, you may come in," a nurse said, holding

open the door to the examination area of the clinic.

Jack slowly rose from his chair.

"Do you need help?" the nurse asked as Ken moved to help Jack.

"Thanks. I can make it on my own," Jack said weakly.

The nurse and Ken had just helped Jack onto the examination table when Doctor Knight entered the room. Ken stood at the side of the table as the nurse left the room.

"How are we doing, Ken?" the doctor asked.

"So so."

Doctor Knight pulled out an X-ray and placed it on the wall-mounted view box hanging to Ken's right.

"Jack. Ken," the doctor said, pointing to an area of the image of Jack's right upper lung. "That's evidence of a tumor."

Jack's face blanched as pale as a ghost's. For a moment, the room was deadly quiet.

"What kind of tumor?" Jack asked almost in a whisper.

Ken gripped Jack's hand.

"Yeah, Doctor," Ken said. "What kind?"

Doctor Knight looked back at the X-ray. "I'm afraid it's not good . . . a carcinoma . . . a cancer."

Jack shook his head and looked at the floor for a second, then at Ken, and then the doctor. "Shit! Can you treat it, Doc? Please, say it's treatable. Tell me I've got many more years. I have too many things I want to do to have cancer."

"Please, sit down, Ken," the doctor said and then faced Jack. "First, I would like to do some more tests. Make sure it hasn't spread."

"What if it has?" Jack asked. "On second thought, I don't know if I want to hear your answer or not."

"If it has, then we'll have to consider other therapies than what I'm thinking of now."

"Can you cut it out? Tell me you can. Tell me you can get rid of it . . . completely."

"Right now . . . I'm not sure. I don't think so, but if it has spread, we can use radiation and chemotherapy."

Ken sat quietly, rubbing his thumbs and forefingers together. He wondered if he should ask how long Jack had. *Better not.*

Ken coughed, looked at the doctor, and asked, "When can we get the other tests?"

"How about day after tomorrow?"

"Where?" Ken asked.

"Meet you guys in the outpatient department at Mountain Top Hospital at 9 a.m."

Jack and Ken made their way down the stairs of their Victorian style home.

"Do we need to slow down?" Ken asked, helping Jack step-by-step.

"A little," Jack said. "Let me sit in the living room for a few minutes."

"Rest here. I'll bring the car around, while you catch your breath."

Jack inhaled deeply and then began to cough. He reached for a tissue in his pocket. Clearing his mouth, he stared at a lump of yellow phlegm containing several small blood clots.

Just then, Ken returned. "Are you ready?"

"Yeah, I'm ready, but I coughed up blood again."

Ken visibly swallowed hard and then took a deep breath. "Well, we'll tell Doctor Knight. Let me help you up."

"Why are these examination rooms always so

cold?" Jack asked.

"I hadn't noticed," Ken replied, feeling anxious.

"What do you think he's going to tell us?"

"I hope it's good news," Ken mumbled.

The examination room door opened and Doctor Knight entered. "Gentlemen. How have you been these past few days, Jack?"

"So so."

"Doctor," Ken said, "he coughed up some blood clots today."

"Hmm," the doctor said, opening Jack's medical record. "You did?"

"Yeah. What have you found out?" Jack asked, his voice quivering.

Doctor Knight placed an X-ray on the view-box and pointed at different spots on the film. "Looks like it has spread . . . here and here."

A tear trickled down Jack's cheek. "And . . . What does that mean?"

"Surgery is out of the question." The doctor stared Jack in the eye. "We can offer you some relief by using chemotherapy and radiation therapy focused on the larger tumors."

"Will my hair fall out?"

"Yes, but it *will* grow back," Doctor Knight said reassuringly. "It takes about six weeks."

"Anything else we have to worry about?" Ken asked, squeezing Jack's hand.

"Chemo often causes GI upsets. There may be some nausea, vomiting, and diarrhea."

"I know about that," Jack said. "My friend, Martin, had chemo."

"How well did he handle it?" Doctor Knight asked.

"He died," Jack said tersely.

"Sorry," Doctor Knight said then handed Ken some pamphlets about cancer therapies. "Read these. You and Jack discuss the material. If you have any questions give me a call. Jack, I'd like to get the chemo started Monday."

"We'll be there," Jack said, nodding and squeezing Ken's hand. *God help me stay strong . . . for Ken's sake.*

Chapter 4

Ken loved working in his small garden. Jack took great pleasure in its beauty from the back patio while sipping a Margarita and watching Ken weed his plants.

The Saturday before Jack's chemo started, Ken busied himself with the care of his tomato plants. Pulling weeds and snipping dead leaves allowed him to escape worry about Jack that filled his soul.

As usual, Jack sat on the patio sipping a Margarita. "Hey, Ken. Don't stay out there too long. It's a scorcher, and I don't want you getting a heat stroke. Did you put on your sun screen?"

"Thanks for your worry," Ken said and straightened up. He wiped sweat from beneath his broad brimmed straw hat. "I'll . . . be . . . in . . . innn . . . in . . . fiv . . . min—"

Jack, resting on a patio lounge, sat upright and stared at Ken. "Are you alright?"

Mouth open, Ken stared blankly. He seemed confused—lost. His eyes were wide and filled with fear. "I . . . don't . . . kno . . . "

Jack waved. "Ken, you aren't making sense. Get in out of the sun."

Ken wondered what was happening to him.

Oh God. *My tongue and right leg don't work. I'm having a stroke. Damn it, a stroke. Gotta get help. Now. God don't let me die. Please don't let me die. Jack, come get me.*

"Ken. Are you okay?" Jack called.

Ken said nothing but erratically waved his left hand to beckon Jack.

"Shit!" Jack said then rushed to Ken's side. "I'm coming, buddy. I'm coming."

Ken staggered a bit. He almost fell but managed to grab Jack's arm just as he arrived.

"What's wrong?" Jack asked, fear coloring his voice.

Ken's fear-filled eyes stared at his lover, his lip quivering as he gripped Jack's arm. "M . . . y ton . . . gue does . . . n't . . . wo . . . rk."

"Oh God!" you're having a stroke. Got to get you to the hospital."

"Ca . . . ll am . . . bul . . . an . . . ce," Ken stuttered as his weight fell against Jack.

"Oh God, you've got to walk to the car. I don't want to wait for an ambulance. I'll drive."

"He . . . lp me."

"Don't worry. We'll take care of this."

Jack's lips moved silently as he prayed, *God don't let him die, not now, not here. I need him . . . beside me. I can't live without him. We have so much to do. So many places to go, so many things to see . . . do. Leave him here, God. Here. Right here with me. Help me get him help. Help me God. Help me.*

Despite the heat and his weakness, Ken mustered the strength to drag himself, with Jack's help, to the car. Jack managed to push and pull his lover onto the passenger seat and then ran into the house to get the keys.

When he returned, Ken had slumped in the seat. Jack stared in disbelief at his lover and burst into tears. "Don't you dare die here."

Opening Ken's door, Jack felt for a pulse. Fortunately, Ken managed to grip Jack's hand but said nothing.

"Thank, God!" Jack shouted, closing the door and then running to the driver's side of the car.

Jack drove eighty miles an hour through his neighborhood. Once on the highway, he accelerated to a hundred miles an hour. He turned on his emergency blinker lights and blew the horn at anything that came close to getting in his way.

Finally, he pulled into the parking area of the emergency room just as a three man EMT ambu-lance crew was about to leave after unloading a patient. Jack yelled to the men as he ran to Ken's door. "Stroke. Help me. He's having a stroke."

One of the EMTs went for a stretcher and returned with it and a nurse. Another EMT put a blood pressure cuff on Ken and the other stood by to help load him onto the stretcher.

"Blood pressure is 180 over 68," one EMT said.

"Great," the nurse said, checking his pulse. "Get him on the stretcher. I'll get a doctor to see him right away. Take him to bay three.

Suddenly, Jack felt faint. Panting, he leaned against his car's fender, placed his hands on his knees, and inhaled deeply.

A nurse stood at the emergency room door holding it open for Ken's entry. When she saw Jack leaning against the car, she ran to his side. "Are you okay?"

"Just . . . tired. Exhausted."

"I'll get a wheelchair. Wait right there."

In seconds, the nurse returned with a wheelchair. She seated jack and then pushed him into an examin-ation bay and checked his blood pressure and pulse.

The harsh smell of alcohol and disinfectant cut Jack's breath short.

"Do you have any health problems?" the nurse asked, putting an oxygen mask over Jack's mouth and nose.

"Lung cancer. I'm supposed to start chemo on

Monday. How's my Ken?"

"Your Ken?"

"Yes. We're married. I think he's having a stroke."

"Doctor Knight is with him now. If Ken is having a stroke, you got him to the right place. We have twenty-four hour a day specialists to care for stroke patients. If we see them within an hour of onset, we can prevent a lot of problems."

"Good," Jack said and sighed loudly. *Thank God.* "His problem started about twenty minutes ago."

"Then I'm sure he'll be fine. You relax and keep the mask on. I'll be back in a minute."

Jack could hear Ken's doctors and nurses in the curtain-surrounded exam bay next to his.

"We need to get him to radiology and the angio lab right away," a bass sounding male voice said.

"Who can give permission?"

"He's married to Jack in the next bay," a woman said.

"Good. I'll talk to Jack," the man said.

Seconds later, Jack's cubicle curtain parted, and in walked a tall, good looking blond man in a long white coat. "Jack, I'm Doctor Knight. How are you doing?"

Jack lifted the plastic oxygen mask off his face.

"Much better with this oxygen. I have lung cancer, and I'm supposed to start chemo Monday."

"Sorry to hear that," the doctor said and then bit his upper lip. "I've just finished examining Ken. I believe he's having a stroke. It's early, and I think we can stop most of its effect, if we act quickly."
"What do you need to do?"

"First we need to do a CAT scan of his head, see if we can identify the site. We may also do a procedure where we insert a catheter, a kind of thin tube, from his groin up his aorta, and into the left-brain artery. Then we inject a special dye to outline the blood vessels and further define the problem. Depending on what we find, we'll give him a blood thinner to dissolve any clots we find." The doctor put his foot on the footstool at the edge of the bed. "The thinner could lead to major bleeding problems in the GI tract or the brain. While that's a possibility, it's not very probable. Does Ken have any GI problems, bleeding or kidney problems?"

"No. He's been pretty healthy until now, except for diabetes. He's not very compliant with his diet or taking his insulin." Jack repositioned himself on the bed. "When are you going to do Ken's tests?"

"With your permission, right away. Will you give permission . . . sign the permit?"

"Absolutely."

"Good. Someone will get the required papers to you shortly."

"Can I see him?"

As Jack attempted to sit up, Doctor Knight helped him. "Are you steady on your feet," he asked.

"Yeah. I'm okay."

The doctor removed Jack's oxygen mask. "Let me help you to Ken's bay."

Jack was greeted with the whir and beeps of several machines as he entered Ken's treatment area. Ken's left eyelid and the left corner of his mouth drooped.

"Is he awake?" Jack asked.

"He is, but he's a little confused. That's not unusual."

Jack took Ken's hand and kissed him on the forehead. Ken opened his eyes just enough to see

Jack. His right hand squeezed Jack's as he struggled to smile a half-smile.

Chapter 5

Feeling better, Jack paced the waiting room while waiting for information on Ken's condition. Jack's anxiety crowded out the chatter coming from the corner television, which was ignored by other anxious people awaiting information about their relatives.

Soon, Jack tired and sat in a chair. After three or four minutes he resumed pacing.

An eternity later, Ken's doctor entered the waiting room to speak to Jack.

"Let's sit in the corner," the doctor said, helping Jack to a seat. "Everything went well. I believe we dissolved the clot. You got him here quickly after the stroke's onset, so I expect all of his neurological functions to return. He should be in his room in a couple of hours and you can see him then."

A tear found its way down Jack's cheek as he sank back in his chair. In a trembling voice, he said, "Thank you, Doctor. Thank you." *Thank you, God!*

"Glad I could help, but you have to make sure he sticks to his diet and takes his insulin as ordered by his primary care doctor." Doctor Knight stared Jack in the eye. "As a diabetic, he's prone to heart attacks, kidney disease, strokes, and high blood pressure."

"Ken is very stubborn about his diet or taking medicine, Doctor, but I'll try."

"He has some carotid artery plaques . . . That's a rough spot in the neck arteries where clots could form or pieces of one could break off and travel to his brain. If that happens, he could have another stroke, so he's going to need anticoagulants to prevent more clots from forming."

"As dangerous as this one?" Jack asked.

"Possibly, but he could also have 'little strokes too.'"

"What's that?" Jack asked, shrugging and turning his palms to the ceiling.

"They're usually transient episodes of confusion, slurred speech, and physical instability."

"Would I be able to see them or tell if he's having one?"

"Probably, but if he acts strangely, has any confusion, or has difficulty speaking, have him seen right away."

"Don't worry, Doc. I will."

"Have him seen by your family doctor in a few days." Doctor Knight closed Ken's medical record. "Well, if you don't have any more questions, I'll be on my way."

"Thanks, Doc." *Thank you God!*

Chapter 6

"It's nice to be home," Ken said, scanning his expansive backyard from a chair on the back patio. "You did a   nice job of keeping my flowers going. Watered them a lot I guess."

"I had to." Jack chuckled, "I didn't want you and them dying at the same time."

"I guess I was in a bad way, huh?"

"Let's just say I was concerned." Jack sipped his iced tea. "Doc says you have to be very mindful of your diabetes. Take your insulin."

"I guess that means no more gins and tonics, huh?"

"Gin is okay, but we have to find you some sugar free tonic water."

A week later, Ken said, "Jack. We have to get you scheduled for your chemo. I'm feeling pretty good these days, and I can take care of the house while we work on getting you better."

Looking dejected, Jack stared at Ken. "I don't look forward to it, but I guess it has to be done. I know the damn stuff will make me feel like shit. It'll probably wipe me out." Jack sighed then said, "I don't know if I can go through with it." *Who'll look in on you . . . make sure you're okay. I can't take care of you while I'm on that shit.*

"I took the liberty of contacting Doctor Knight the other day," Ken said, "and he's scheduled you to start chemo on Monday."

"In two days?"

"Yes. Monday. I'll drive you. I can do it. I'm feeling much better."

"Maybe we should get James to drive us."

"Don't be ridiculous. He's working. How is he going to get time off to chauffer us? No, I'll drive."

For the rest of the weekend, Jack felt anxious about his upcoming date with chemotherapy. He had difficulty sleeping and lost his appetite.

Monday morning, Jack reluctantly forced himself from bed.

"Breakfast is ready," Ken yelled from the kitchen.

"Coming."

Jack sat at the table and stared at his dry toast. "What's this?"

"Doctor said you shouldn't have a heavy greasy meal this morning. Use that artificial, spray stuff. It tastes like butter."

"No coffee?"

"No," Ken said, scrambling two eggs for himself. "Have a glass of that 1% milk."

Wrinkling his face with a smirk, Jack said, "I don't have to worry about cancer killing me. I'll starve to death."

"Eat up. We have to leave soon."

At the infusion clinic, the nurse greeted the men then looked at Jack's wrist band. "Your first chemo session?"

"Yeah. First one," Jack mumbled.

"Have a seat here," the nurse said, pointing to a reclining lounge chair. "I'll get my supplies and be right back."

Jack sat in the cushy, fake-leather recliner and surveyed his surroundings. He could see the feet of four other chemo patients sticking past the colorful curtains that separated each patient's treatment area. One patient's feet jerked about as their owner intermittently wretched.

"Not going too well for that guy," Jack said to Ken.

Ken patted Jack's hand and then squeezed it. "But you won't have that problem."

The nurse returned with an armful of plastic and liquid things.

"Is all that for me?" Jack asked.

"It is," the nurse said. "The fluids are the first step to your cure."

Jack extended his arm so the nurse could tie a tourniquet around his bicep. "Grip your hand a few times," she said. "Okay, you'll feel a little stick. Good. The needle is in."

The nurse taped the needle in place and then adjusted the flow of the IV fluid. She watched silently as it dripped inside a small clear plastic cylinder then slowly flowed into Jack's vein. "If you have any untoward symptoms," she said, "push this call button. One of the nurses will respond to see what we can do to help."

Ken looked up from a patient pamphlet he had been reading. "Says here we can watch TV, listen to music with those headphones, or you can read. Do you have a preference?"

"If I listen to music, what will you do?" Jack asked.

"I'll read."

"Okay. Would you hand me the headphones? Thanks."

An hour later, Jack stirred from a nap. "I think I'm feeling a little nauseous."

Ken pushed the help button. Seconds later a nurse arrived. "What's happening men?"

"Jack is feeling nauseous."

"Take some deep breaths through your mouth and try to relax," the nurse said, handing Jack an emesis basin then headed for the door. "I'll get something to help make that nauseous feeling go away."

Just then Jack had a large retch and lost his skimpy breakfast.

"Oh my," the nurse said, wetting a washcloth then wiping Jack's face.

She glanced at Ken. "You watch him while I get some medication."

In a flash, the nurse was back and injected several drops of clear liquid in Jack's IV tubing. "There. That should help."

In a matter of minutes, Jack felt better. He stared at the empty bottle hanging above his head. "Well, one down and a thousand more to go."

"I heard that," the nurse said, entering Jack's treatment space. "Time to get you out of here."

"We're ready to leave," Ken said, a note of seriousness tingeing his words.

Ken got Jack settled in the car and then headed for home. Just as the car entered the exit ramp of I-95, Jack began to retch.

"Better pull over," Jack said.

"Hold on," Ken said, bringing the car to a halt on the narrow shoulder near the foot of the ramp.

Jack opened his door and hurriedly exited the car, ready to vomit. Bent over with his hands on his knees, he looked back at Ken sitting behind the steering wheel. He appeared to stare into space.

"Ken! Ken! Are you alright?"

"Huh?" Ken mumbled.

"What's wrong?" Jack yelled.

"What's wrong?" Ken repeated.

"Look at me," Jack yelled. "Look at me!"

Slowly, Ken looked at Jack. "Dooooo yooooou neeeed help?" Ken asked, his speech slurred.

Without waiting for Jack to answer, Ken opened his door and exited the car. Suddenly, the car began to roll down the ramp. Ken had failed to put the car in park, set the parking brake, or turn off the ignition.

Ken seemed rooted in concrete—dazed. He watched his Volvo, both front doors open, roll down the ramp.

Jack looked on in horror and started to run after the car when he experienced an over powering wave of nausea followed by explosive vomiting. As he vomited, he noted a Mercedes entering the exit ramp at a high rate of speed. Forcing himself upright, Jack waved at the driver and weakly yelled, "Stop! Stop!"

The driver must have thought Jack was a hitchhiker wanting a ride because the driver looked briefly at Jack and continued down the ramp.

"Ken! Get out of the way!" Jack yelled and closed his eyes. Just then, Jack slipped. He fell on the safety rail at the side of the ramp, opening a laceration on his forehead.

With a screech sounding like fighting cats, the air filled with the shriek of skidding tires and the odor of burning rubber. The sounds and smells were followed by crunching sounds associated with a car recycling press heard only in junkyards. Suddenly, a deafening calm blanketed the ramp.

Jack mustered the courage to open his eyes. He saw Ken slumped against the right ramp's guard rail and the Mercedes wedged in the side of the Ken's Volvo, which had been pushed to the bottom of the ramp.

Jack quickly scanned Ken and the area around

him for blood. *Thank God he's not bleeding. Mine is enough.*

Jack made his way to Ken's side and stared him in the eye. "Speak to me! Say something."

Ken stared silently into space.

The driver of a Camaro, exiting the highway, saw the carnage and stopped beside Ken and Jack.

"You guys alright?" the stranger asked.

"No," Jack replied. "We need an ambulance. My partner is having a stroke. I just have a cut on my forehead."

"What about the other car?" the stranger asked.

"I don't know," Jack replied and looked toward the Mercedes.

"Look," the stranger said, "someone is getting out of the Mercedes." The stranger tossed his cell phone to Jack and said, "Call 911 and I'll check on that driver."

The driver's door of the Mercedes opened wider. A short, white haired man, pulling at the airbag caught on the door handle, slowly exited the car. The man stood erect and brushed glass shards from his jacket and pants.

"You okay?" the driver of the Camaro asked the elderly Mercedes' driver.

"I think so," the man said. "Just shook up. I don't see any blood except for a few drops from these small cuts on my hand and forehead."

The elderly driver looked up the ramp toward Ken. "That son of a bitch was walking right in the middle of the ramp. Glad I missed him. What the hell was he thinking?"

The Camaro driver said, "The guy with the bleeding forehead said the man leaning on the guardrail is having a stroke. I gave them my phone to call 911."

The stranger stared at the crushed Volvo. "Who's in the Volvo?"

"God only knows," the elderly man said. "When I first saw the car, both its doors were open, and it was rolling down the ramp. I couldn't stop fast enough to avoid it."

"Strange," the Camaro driver said, walking toward the Volvo.

The Mercedes' impact had knocked the driver's door off the Volvo's frame and caused the passenger door to close. The Camaro driver looked all around the interior of the Volvo. "What the fuck," the Camaro driver said to the elderly driver. "The car is empty. No driver. No passengers. Nobody."

"Can't be," the elderly man said. "How the hell does an empty car get on an exit ramp?"

An ambulance came to a screeching stop on the ramp, bringing Jack back to reality as the ambulance siren whined down.

Within minutes, Ken and Jack were in the ambulance and on their way to the hospital.

Jack stared at the EMT monitoring Ken's EKG.

"Is it okay?" Jack asked.

"So far," the EMT said.

Minutes later, the EMT said, "We're here." He rechecked Ken's blood pressure.

The rear doors of the ambulance opened and two EMTs pulled Ken's stretcher from the vehicle.

The EMTs pushed the stretcher into the emergency room as the third EMT held an infusing bottle of IV fluids.

"A stroke," the lead EMT said to a nurse. He headed to a treatment bay pointed to by the nurse who joined the train of people handling the gurney.

"We've been monitoring your telemetry," the nurse said to the lead EMT. "His EKG recordings have been stable. That's a good sign."

The emergency room secretary handed the nurse a few pages of Ken's record. "I printed the reports from the patient's last admission."

Doctor Knight entered the bay and scanned the patient's face. "Do I know you?" the doctor asked as the nurse handed him Ken's old medical records.

Jack interrupted. "You've seen him before, Doc. He's having another stroke."

Doctor Knight did a brief neurological exam and then smiled.

"How is he, Doctor," Jack asked, feeling his wrinkled face sagging from fear.

"Looks like he's had a transient vasospastic event—possibly due to micro-embolism from a neck artery."

"I remember you saying something like that could happen when he was here weeks ago. Is he going to be okay?"

"I think so. Looks like his problem is already starting to recede. See, the droop in his lip is improving."

"You mean that?" Jack asked.

"I do," the doctor said, rechecking Ken's neurological findings. "Nevertheless, we need to keep him for twenty-four hours to make sure there is no worsening of his condition."

Jack took a deep breath and then smiled. "That's the best news I've had in years."

"As I recall, you were undergoing chemo for a lung tumor," Doctor Knight said, looking inquisitively at Jack.

"You have a good memory."

"How is it going?"

"About as good as it could go, I guess."

"Has Ken been taking a baby aspirin every day?"

"I think so. He can be stubborn about medicines, but I think so."

"This is the second episode for him?" the doctor said, flipping through Ken's records.

"Yeah, afraid it is."

"Well, I think we need to start a different anti-coagulant," Doctor Knight said, looking at a list of Ken's medications—something to prevent clots in his vascular system. It's a pill called warfarin or Coumadin."

"I've heard of that. A friend of ours takes it for a problem with his leg arteries."

"It's probably the same medication," The doctor said, closing Ken's records. "Coumadin requires periodic blood testing to make sure the correct dosage is being used. Other than that, I don't anticipate any problems."

Doctor Knight stopped talking, tilted his head, and listened intently. "I think I'm being paged. I have to answer it, but I'll write orders for Ken. We'll keep him in the ER for a while. If all goes well, he'll be discharged tomorrow."

Chapter 7

"Ready to go home?" Jack asked.

"The sooner the better," Ken said, taking off his reading glasses.

Moments later, a nurse entered and instructed Ken on the care plan he should adhere to at home.

Ken signed his discharge papers and left the hospital in a wheelchair pushed by a nurse's aide to his car.

He was silent as he stared out the passenger window at the passing scenery.

"You feeling okay?" Jack asked, looking away from the road.

"Yeah. Just thinking about how forgetful I've become."

"That's one of the reasons you have to faithfully take your medicines. Doc says the new medicine could cause serious bleeding if you don't do every-thing you're supposed to do."

"Yeah. Yeah. Yeah."

"I'm serious. You have to follow doctor's orders. I don't want you up and dying on me."

"I promise not to die on you."

Ken tuned the car radio to the classical music station from New York. "Oh, I love that melody. Vivaldi is one of my favorite composers."

Jack slowed the car and turned onto their street.

"It feels so good to be back in our own neighbor-hood," Ken said. "I love these Cedar trees."

"I'm glad you're back," Jack said. "Let's get you settled in."

Ken went to the bedroom, fluffed up his pillow, and stretched out on the bed while Jack went to the kitchen to prefill Ken's medicine box with a week's worth of pills.

Entering the bedroom, Jack said, "I've filled your medicine box for each day, so there's no excuse for you not taking your pills."

"Thanks. I won't forget."

Life for the two men continued without major incidents. However, there were times when Jack thought Ken might be having staring spells, but if he did, they didn't last long.

Jack finished his chemotherapy and was happy to know his tumor had shrunk significantly. Unfortunately, it had not disappeared.

On a follow up visit to his doctor, Ken let Jack out of the car at the clinic door then drove away to park the car.

"How's your appetite," Doctor Kim asked Jack during his follow-up visit at the clinic.

"I've been eating quite well, thank you," Jack said. "Even put on a few pounds since I finished the poisons." He rubbed his almost bald head. "Even my hair is starting to sprout."

"That's good, but I'll need to see you every two weeks for a while, get some X-rays of your chest and monitor your blood counts."

Doctor Kim turned to Ken. "You men stop at the appointment desk and schedule your next visit. I'll see you then."

In the east end of the clinic parking lot, Ken looked around for his car. "Now where did I park the damn car?"

"Push the remote button," Jack said, "that'll cause the horn to blow."

Ken pushed the button. A distant beep sounded in the far west side of the lot.

"God, the car is way over there, Ken." *His memory is really getting bad!*

Sweating from heat and humidity, the men got in the car. Ken started the engine and headed for the lot exit. At the guard house, Ken handed the validated ticket to the guard and drove slowly to the middle of the street and then stopped.

"Ken," Jack said, "traffic is clear in both directions. What are you waiting for?" Jack stared at Ken. "Ken, what are you waiting for? Let's go."

After a moment of silence, Ken said, "I don't remember where we live."

"Oh God, Ken. Turn right." *Jesus, help us. What am I going to do with him? He'll get angry if I tell him he can't drive anymore.*

Slowly, Ken turned right, crept to the intersection, and stopped at a red traffic light. When the light turned green, Ken looked left and right but didn't move the car. Several cars behind him blew their horns.

"For God's sake, Ken, turn left. Left!"

Ken turned left and drove at five miles per hour. Suddenly, he burst out crying.

Alarmed, Jack asked, "What's wrong?"

Through his sobs, Kens said, "I don't know where I'm going."

"Pull into that driveway on the right and stop the car."

Ken did as instructed.

Jack went to Ken's side of the car and opened his door. "Get out, buddy."

Ken slowly exited the car and stood beside the open door.

"Let me see you smile," Jack said, taking Ken's face in his hands. "Good. There's no droop. Now stick out your tongue . . . that's good. Now close your eyes."

Ken's body swayed slightly, but he did not fall.

Jack said, "With your eyes closed, touch your nose with an index finger and then extend your arm then repeat with the other finger."

Slowly, Ken did as instructed.

"Thank God," Jack said. "Everything is like it was when Doctor Knight examined you. Get in on the passenger's side; I'll drive us home."

Jack drove silently, periodically staring at Ken and worrying. Jack thought about what Ken's doctor had said about the possibility of a slow, steady loss of memory due to repeated "little" strokes.

"I remember this place," Ken said, as Jack drove into their driveway. "This is home."

"How are you feeling this morning, Jack?" Doctor Smyth asked.

"I feel tired all the time," Jack said. "I've been having a little blood in my sputum, and my appetite isn't worth shit."

"Yeah," Ken said. "He hardly eats anything, and he gets short of breath easily."

"Sorry to hear that," Doctor Smyth said, sliding an X-ray onto a lighted view-box. "Jack . . . I'm sorry to tell you that your tumor is growing again." The doctor pointed at a spot on the X-ray.

"I'm not surprised. I suspected that."

"The tumor is growing into the upper lobe of your left lung." Doctor Smyth put an earlier chest X-ray on the view box for a side by side comparison. "See there. This was seven months ago."

Doctor Smyth silently faced Jack who apparent-ly waited for a response.

"I had a feeling something was wrong." Jack said then took a deep breath. Is there anything you can do?" *Please say yes. Please.*

"We could give you another round of chemo. I'm not sure how much it will do, but it's worth trying. We can add some radiation as well."

The doctor removed the X-rays from the view box and pushed them into their folder. "Is the combination something you'd like to try?"

"I guess I have to," Jack mumbled, staring at the floor. "Seems there's nothing else—right?"

"There might be some experimental therapies we could explore, but I wouldn't recommend that route until we try another round of standard chemo."

"When do we start? Monday?"

"That'll work. I'll make the arrangements for Monday."

Jack stared at the phone for a few seconds. He then picked up the handset and dialed several numbers.

"Roger, this is Jack. How're you doing?"

"I should be asking you that," Roger said.

"Well, things aren't going so well."

"Sorry to hear that. Anything I can do?"

"There is. I need to start chemo again . . ."

"And . . . "

"I need someone to drive me to the clinic for a few weeks. Ken is so forgetful I can't rely on him not to get lost."

"Jack, you know I'll help. When do we start?"

"I start Monday, eight o'clock. You can drive my car."

"Don't worry about that. We'll get you taken care of. See ya Monday—say 7:15."

Chapter 8

"Doctor Smyth, this is my friend Roger," Jack said, shaking his doctor's hand. "Roger is my driver for the next few weeks."

"Nice to meet you, Roger. Thanks for driving Jack. His partner is having his own health problems." Doctor Smyth glanced at Jack. "Shall we get started?"

A nurse put her hand on Jack's shoulder and pointed to a brown leather recliner. "Please make yourself comfortable, Jack," she said, pulling up a side chair for Roger. "You guys make yourself comfortable. I'll be back in a few minutes."

Moments later the nurse returned. "Okay, I need to start some fluids."

"Yeah, I know about that," Jack said. *I don't want to do this, but what choice do I have?* He closed his eyes while the nurse inserted the needle. "Ouch."

The nurse started the IV infusion. "You're receiving the same chemo you had before. You know what to expect. Use the call button is there's any problem."

"Okay," Jack said and smiled.

The nurse positioned the call button for Jack's access.

"Good. Let me know if you need anything."

Roger watched the drip, drip, drip of the clear fluid inside the three-inch-long, clear plastic chamber just below the container holding the liquid chemo.

Apparently trying to take Jack's mind off his situation, Roger asked, "How's Ken doing?"

"I wish I knew," Jack answered, opening his eyes and looking at Roger. "He doesn't complain, and he doesn't take his medicines. The more I try to get him to take them the more he fights me. I don't know what to do."

"What does his doctor have to say?"

"Ha. I can't get him to see his doctor. When I mention the doctor, Ken says he's 'doing fine—doesn't need to see a doctor.'"

Two hours later, the nurse stepped inside Jack's curtained area. "How is everything going? Any problems?"

"Just a little nausea, but I'm used to that."

"Okay." The nurse counted the chemo drops per minute as Jack and Roger watched her. "Good," she said, smiled, and then left.

Jack looked at Roger, shook his head, and then let it fall back against the recliner. "I can't get Ken to eat. Well, not what he should eat. I'm concerned about his high blood sugar. He's not taking his diabetes medicine."

"Ken's a big boy," Roger said, putting down a magazine. "You need to take care of yourself."

Jack moved his recliner into the upright position and sighed. "I know I'm not going to be around long." He paused speaking and looked at the ceiling. "Maybe twelve months—*if* I'm lucky." He looked at Roger. "Fifteen, if I'm really lucky." Jack teared up and cleared his throat. "Ken's an only child. The last of his relatives, an aunt, died five years ago. He has no one except me, and I worry about what will happen to him when I'm gone. I hate to admit it, but I've prayed we die together. I wouldn't have to worry then."

"Do you guys have a living will or a legal will?"

"We have both, but who would take care of him when I'm no longer around?"

"What about your sister, Linda?"

"Nah. She lives in California," Jack said, shaking his head. "While she likes Ken, I can't expect her to take him in. He'd drive her crazy." Suddenly, Jack's face morphed into a smile then he chuckled, "Like he drives me crazy sometimes."

Roger smiled and then asked, "And Ken's finances?"

"Fortunately, he has long term care insurance. They wouldn't sell it to me when we applied. He also has some trust fund money, his social security, and a pension."

"Maybe you should consider having the trust-fund officer become his steward or legal guardian."

The nurse entered and interrupted the conversation. "Looks like the chemo is finished, Jack. Let's get you disconnected and out of here."

As the nurse removed the needle, Jack looked at Roger. "Thanks for the advice."

Chapter 9

Ken answered the phone. "Ken here."

"Hi, Ken. It's me, Roger."

"Oh, hi. Wait I'll call Jack . . ."

"Hi Roger," Jack said. "Sorry I couldn't get to the phone first."

"No problem. Sunday, you don't have chemo. How would you and Ken like to join me for lunch with some of our mutual friends?"

"Sounds good." *How did he know I needed to get out?* "I'd like to do something besides visit that damn hospital."

"Okay. I'll pick you guys up Sunday at eleven."

Having parked in Mary's Restaurant parking lot, Roger went to Jack's side of the car. "Let me help you out."

"Thanks, Rog. I need it."

Jack stood at the side of the car waiting for Ken to exit the vehicle. After a moment, Jack bent over, tapped Ken's car window then motioned to him to get out.

Ken rolled down his window. "What?"

"It's time to get out," Jack said.

"Where are we?"

"We're at Mary's, your favorite gay restaurant and bar."

"Oh. What are we doing here?"

"Oh, Ken. We're going to have lunch. Please, get out of the car."

Ken seemed to force himself out of his seat, closed the door, and then stood beside the car.

Jack stared at him for a moment then hugged him

and quietly mumbled, "Oh, Ken." *He's getting worse.*

Jack noted a tear rolling down Roger's cheek as he rubbed his eyes. *Roger must be thinking that neither of us guys is going to be around much longer.* "Okay, guys, let's go in, Jack said.

The long, narrow paneled bar was packed with Sunday diners. The establishment was an intergenerational kind of place filled with well-built young men in running gear or Bermuda shorts. A few men wore sports jackets or suits. Two octogenarians, with walkers, seemed unconcerned about making any kind of fashion statement, mixed plaid and stripes.

The room was filled with laughter and light banter buoyed by Abba music playing in the background. Three silent TV sets were tuned to sporting events with captions for those interested in the game.

Jack led Ken toward a group of friends in the back. They waved on seeing the three newcomers enter the bar.

"Hey guys," Jack said, waving on seeing familiar faces.

Eddie, a retired Catholic priest, was first to shake Jack's hand. "Jack, its been a long time since I've seen you. How is the chemo going?"

"You looking to sell a funeral mass?" Jack asked and then smiled. "It's never fun, but hey, what can I do?" *What can anyone do in my circumstances?*

"Well, I've been praying for you and Ken," Eddie said and extended his hand toward Ken. "How are you doing, Ken?"

"Oh, okay," Ken replied.

"What would you guys like to drink?" Roger asked Jack and Ken.

"I'll have a club soda and cranberry juice," Jack said.

"A gin and tonic," Ken said.

"Okay, I'll be right back," Roger said, waving to Kenny, the bartender.

Jack became engaged in conversation with old friends, Bill and Harry, from central Jersey.

Ken looked around while silently waiting for his drink.

"Ken looks like he has lost fifty pounds," Bill whispered in Jack's ear. "What's going on?"

"I don't know," Jack said mournfully, pushing Ken's shirttail into his baggy pants. "He won't take his medicine, he's not eating, and he won't let me take him to his doctor."

"Here we go guys," Roger said, handing over their drinks. Roger touched his glass to theirs and said, "To good health."

"To good health," Jack said.

"Maybe we should go to our table," Bill whispered to Harry. "Jack doesn't look strong enough to stand very long."

"I heard that," Jack said, "but you're right. I'd like to sit down."

"Listen up guys," Harry said, waving his hand toward his other friends, "we're going to go to our table."

Jack ordered southern fried chicken and Ken ordered a hamburger, fries, a bowl of chili, and another gin and tonic.

Jack stared at Ken disapprovingly and then spoke to the waitress. "Cancel everything he ordered except for the chili. I'll be surprised if he eats half of it."

"Oh yes I will," Ken said, appearing perturbed.

"If you eat all the chili," Jack said, "you can

order something else."

Halfway through the meal, Ken left for the bathroom. In a few minutes he returned with his fly open.

Roger smiled then asked, "You trolling for tricks, Ken?"

"What?" Ken asked.

Jack reached out to close Ken's fly, but he interrupted and zipped it himself. He sat down and then reached for a dinner roll.

"Eat your chili first," Jack said, admonishing Ken.

"I will . . . a little later."

The group's conversation was directed to things that had nothing to do with Ken, Jack, or health matters. After twenty minutes, Ken left for the bathroom again.

Bill nudged Jack's elbow. "What's with Ken's frequent bathroom visits? Does he have a trick in there?"

"It's his diabetes. His blood sugar is out of control."

"How high is it?"

"Right now, I don't know. He won't take a reading and he won't let me do one."

"Maybe he'll let me," Bill said. "I have my glucometer in the car,"

"Please, give it a try."

The luncheon ended and everyone headed for the exit. They stood on the front terrace talking about Bill's new car. He went to his car and then returned with his glucometer.

Bill tapped Ken's arm and said, "Let me check your blood sugar."

"No thanks. It's okay," Ken said, putting his

hands behind his back.

"I won't charge anything."

"No thanks."

Jack intervened. "*Ken*, let Bill check your blood sugar."

Ken rolled his eyes. "Okaaaaay."

Bill lanced Ken's middle finger and drew a drop of blood. It flowed onto the paper strip protruding from the glucometer. The blood sugar reading was 538.

Bill placed a piece of tissue over the oozing fingertip and motioned for Jack.

"Ken's blood sugar is on the verge of becoming a serious problem. I suggest you take him directly to a doctor when you leave here."

Jack shook his head. "He won't go inside, even if I take him."

"Do whatever you have to do but get this taken care of."

"Thanks, Bill. I'll see if Roger will help."

At the clinic, Ken asked, "Where are we?"

Roger helped Jack get Ken out of the car. "Ken, you have to see the doctor," Jack said. "Your blood sugar is so high it could kill you in a day or so."

Ken twisted his wrist free of Roger's grip. "How high was it?"

"Five hundred and thirty-eight," Bill replied.

"That's not bad," Ken said and tried to get back in the car.

"Ken, I'm a diabetic, and I know how bad a reading like that is. We're going to see the doctor."

Jack and Roger pulled Ken into the clinic.
After registering, Ken fidgeted in a chair while

waiting for the doctor.

Entering the examination room, the doctor said, "Well, what brings you in today, Ken?"

"These thugs," Ken said, snidely. "I don't need to be here."

"Doctor," Jack said, "his blood sugar is 538."
"On my gosh," the doctor said. "That's pretty high, Ken. I think you should be in the hospital for a day or so until we can get your sugar under control."

"Do admit him," Jack said, pleadingly.

"I don't need no hospital. We can take care of it at home."

"I don't recommend that," the doctor said.

"You're going to the hospital," Jack said. "No if, ands, or buts." Jack turned to the physician. "Doctor, make the arrangements and we'll take him right over."

Two days later, Ken was discharged from the hospital with a new regime of medications.

Unfortunately, he did not follow doctor's orders and often mouthed pills only to spit them out when Jack wasn't looking. Once, Jack caught him and confronted him.

"I don't need those damn pills," Ken complained. "You're trying to poison me."

Feeling frustrated, Jack said, "Listen Ken, I love you dearly, but I can't go on fighting about what you need to do to take care of yourself. Please, help me help you. I want you to live a long time, but you won't if you keep refusing to do what's necessary."
For God's sake, help me Ken.

"You're wrong. I'll be okay without all that crap."

Jack shook his head, slumped into his recliner, and turned on the TV. "Do whatever the hell you want. I'm not fighting anymore."

Later that night, Jack went to bed, feeling exhausted and depressed. After turning and tossing, he finally dropped off to sleep around 2:00 a.m.

Chapter 10

Jack awoke 5:10 a.m., coughing. He sat up and began to cough bright red blood.

"Oh God," Jack said. *Shit! This is serious!* "I've got to get to the hospital."

He got dressed and picked up his car keys and headed for the door. "Shit, I'd better wake Ken. Gotta take him with me. I can't leave him alone."

Over the past year, Ken had started to roam the house at night. For Jack to get any sleep, he and Ken slept in separate rooms.

Jack went to Ken's bedroom and saw light leaking around the door. He knocked on the door and said, "Ken, we have to go to the hospital. I'm coughing blood. Get up and get dressed."

There was no sound from the room. Jack knocked again and waited. Still no answer. He opened the door and saw Ken stretched across the bed, asleep and dressed.

"Thank God, I don't have to dress you."

Jack shook Ken and finally got him up and into the car.

"Why are we going grocery shopping at this hour?" Ken asked.

"There are fewer people in the store at this time, and we get the best bargains now."

"Good. I need some Trident."

"I'll get you four packs."

Jack pulled up to the ER entrance and went to Ken's side of the car.

"Let's go in," Jack said. "I'll get a grocery cart and let you ride in it."

Jack pulled a wheelchair from among several parked outside the ER doors then helped Ken to get in.

Jack pushed the chair inside then stopped at the registration desk.

"Why are we stopping here?" Ken asked.

"I have to ask which aisle your Trident is in."

Jack told the receptionists he was coughing blood and then explained Ken's problem. The clerk was told twice that Ken was not the reason the men were in the ER.

In a short time, Jack was seen by a resident doctor. He ordered several blood tests and a chest X-ray. An hour later, the test reports were available.

The doctor returned to Jack's cubicle just as Ken asked, "Where is the Trident you promised me?"

"Would he settle for a stick of Juicy Fruit Gum?" the doctor asked. "I always carry some."

"I'm sure he would," Jack said.

The doctor handed Ken a stick of gum. Ken took it and then stared at it, "This is okay, but I still want my Trident."

The doctor sat on a stool and rolled it to the side of the examination table on which Jack sat. "Jack, your blood tests show you have some anemia. That may be related to your recent chemotherapy, lack of appetite, and chronic blood loss. The tests indicate no blood related bleeding disorder. However, your chest X-ray doesn't look good. I've compared tonight's film with one done a few weeks ago. There's more tumor. I believe that's the reason you're coughing blood."

Jack was quiet for a moment. *Shit! This is not what I wanted to hear.* He looked at his right fore-finger and thumb rubbing each other. "What do you suggest, Doctor?"

"I'm sorry to say this, but I think you should check into an inpatient hospice program. We can keep you comfortable, but I don't know of anything more we can offer in terms of traditional therapies. You have had all we can offer."

"I can't do that," Jack said, shaking his head. *God, don't let this be true.* "I have responsibilities at home. I'm Ken's caretaker. We've been together for fifty-two years, and I'm not leaving him now."

"I understand," the doctor said. "Maybe we could arrange for hospice homecare. A nurse could make home visits, and we could get an aide in to help with custodial care needs. You know—help bathe you, clean the house, get your pills for you."

"That sounds good. See what you can do, Doc."

"I'll send a message to our social service department. They're the ones who set up home care." The doctor took out a prescription pad. "I'm going to write a prescription for codeine. It's a cough suppressant. It will help curb your coughing spells. Coughing is probably contributing to the bleeding in your lung."

"Thanks," Jack said, pathos coloring his voice. "Anything to help . . . to give me a day or two more."

"How are you going to get home?" the doctor asked.

"I drove myself here, and … I guess I can drive myself home."

Jack signed his discharge papers then prepared to leave. A nurse approached him and said, "Doctor wants you to have this codeine tablet. Take it when you get home. You won't be able to get a prescription filled at this hour but don't take this tablet until you get home."

As Jack pushed the wheelchair carrying Ken to the car, the nurse shook her head and spoke to the doctor. "What a sad case."

"Yeah," the doctor said, "one of the bad sides of getting old. I hope his death is quick and painless."

"How do you think he'll die?"

"If he's lucky, he'll die quickly—a hemorrhage."

Chapter 11

"Yes, I said hospice program?" Maggie repeated to the person at the other end of the line.

"Sorry, I'm new with the hospital's social service department," Janet said.

"I want to set up a home hospice program for one of our patients."

"What is the patient's name?" Janet asked.

Maggie provided the information concerning Jack's diagnosis, insurance coverage, domestic situation, and prognosis.

"Is he expected to live longer than six months?"

"No. His death is expected within six months. That should satisfy the Medicare people, but in reality, he probably has only days maybe a few weeks at most."

"What did the doctor say the terminal event might be?" Janet asked.

"Blood loss. Probably a hemorrhage, so we had better get a load of black towels in the house."

Janet was quiet for a second. "Black? Why black?"

"They don't show blood as much as lighter colored towels."

"Oh God," Janet said. "I don't want to hear about that on my first day."

Two days later, a registered nurse visited Jack and Ken to assess the home situation.

"Do you have any family nearby … for help or support?" she asked.

"I have an older brother about a mile away," Jack said. "I can call him if I have to, but he is not well either."

"I'll need his name, address and phone number before I leave. I think you'll need a nurse for four hours a day. Would you prefer mornings or afternoons?"

Jack glanced at Ken. "Afternoons would be best."

"Then I'll arrange for an aide to be here for four hours in the morning." The nurse looked toward the kitchen. "Do you cook or should we schedule Meals on Wheels to bring in lunch and dinner?"

"Neither of us eats much. I think I can make do. Cooking keeps me busy—helps keep my mind off things. If we need the meals, I'll let you know, and you can arrange them."

"Very well. Your aide will start tomorrow. Her name is Bessy. She should be here around eight thirty. Here's my card. Call me if you think of any-thing else you might need. By the way, did you get your prescription for codeine filled?"

"I did. Just before you came."

"Good. Take care."

Jack had a restless night worrying about Ken. *Who will take care of him after I'm gone.*

Jack's thoughts turned to death. *Is it painful? Will it be quick?* He sat on the side of the bed, head in his hands. *Is there really a heaven or hell? Where am I going? Should I end all this right now? Take Ken with me?*

Jack turned on the bedside lamp, picked up the bottle of codeine tablets then counted them. *Twenty-six are left. If I take one every four hours they'll last only a few days . . . Did that doctor expect me to live only a week or did he not give me more because he thought I might take them all at once—kill myself?*

He poured the pills back into the bottle, turned off the lamp, lay down, and stared into the darkness. He had never known such emptiness nor heard such silence. He tried to clear his mind and then whispered, "God. Are you real? Can you hear me?" For a moment he lay still as though waiting for a voice from on high. "Even if you're real, why would you speak to me? I've never spoken to you . . . well not since mother made me say my prayers. Are you real?"

The vacuum in his heart waited for a surge of divine fulfillment, but it didn't happen. His eyes burned and his eyeballs felt as if they would explode. He fought hard to hold back tears. Nevertheless, a tear crept down his cheek. It was followed by more, and then they flowed from heartache and fear. Jack sobbed in great waves of despair and feelings of loss and abandonment. He wailed saying, "God, help me. Please help me!"

Jack walked into the kitchen at 7:10 a.m. and saw Ken sitting at the table. "Morning, Ken. You're looking good. Sleep okay?"

"Like a baby," Ken said, stirring his tea.

"Glad someone did. I certainly didn't."

The doorbell rang.

"I'll get it," Jack said, leaving for the front door. "It's probably Bessy, the health aide. I'll let her in."

"Morning, Bessy."

"Morning Mister Jack. Did you have a good night?"

"So so."

"Think we can check Mister Ken's blood sugar this morning?" she asked.

"I'll hold his arm and hand, if you do the rest."

The two went to the kitchen where Jack grasped Ken's hand. "Ken, Bessy and I need to check your blood sugar."

"I don't need no damn sugar testing," Ken yelled and tried to wrest his hand free of Jack's grip.

"Hold him," Bessy said, while she lanced Ken's fingertip and then milked a drop of blood from the puncture site. "Hold still," she said as she collected the droplet onto the test strip.

"There. It's done," Bessy said. "The reading is 838. That's bad. I'm surprised he can still function with readings that high. Seizures or unconsciousness can happen at that level."

Jack took Bessy aside. "We've got to get some insulin in him, Bessy."

"You know how hard that's going to be, Mister Jack?

"Let's wait until he's asleep," Jack said. "I'll get the insulin ready and you hold his arms. I'll inject his hip. I just hope I'm strong enough to hold his legs."

"It's worth a try, but maybe you should talk to his doctor about the amount of insulin we should give him."

"Good idea. I'll call him."

Jack phoned Ken's doctor and discussed Ken's situation.

"Ideally, we would give him insulin and IV fluids," the doctor said, "but knowing his mental state, he won't let that happen. See if you can inject a hundred units of insulin then check his blood sugar two to three hours later and let me know the results. You know we could have him committed for three days and treat him if you wanted."

"That would kill him—mentally that is. He would hate me for doing it. No I can't do that."

"Do you still have any of his oral diabetic drugs?"

"Somewhere, I'm sure."

"Find them and then crush them in Ken's favorite food. Give him the medicine throughout the day and let's see how that affects his blood sugar."

"Okay. We'll do that. Thanks Doc."

After breakfast, Ken watched television for a few minutes and then went to his room. Jack helped him remove his robe and get into bed. He wore only briefs.

Thirty minutes later, Jack and Bessy crept into Ken's room. He slept on his left side, facing away from the door. Jack had the insulin syringe at the ready while Bessy lifted the sheet off Ken's lower body.

Jack whispered, "One, two, three."

Bessy grabbed Ken's wrists and Jack grabbed Ken's right leg and then jabbed the needle into Ken's right hip. Ken suddenly broke free of Bessy's grip and slapped at Jack's hand. Jack had managed to push the syringe plunger two thirds of the way down.

"Fuck you," Ken yelled, knocking at the syringe.

Suddenly, insulin sprayed across the sheets instead of ending up in Ken's hip.

Ken jumped from bed. "Get the fuck out of my room!"

For the first time, Ken became belligerent, throwing his fists as if trying to land a punch.

"Let's go, Bessy," Jack said, breathlessly. "He needs to quiet down."

Short of breath, Jack sank into his chair in the living room and began to cry. "What is to become of him, Bessy? I don't know what to do."

"Maybe you should have him committed."

"Oh, God," Jack said shocked. "I couldn't do that. He's aware enough to think I didn't love him anymore or had abandoned him . . . something he has always worried about . . . being alone, unwanted. No. I couldn't do that."

"Then we have to have several people come in every day and hold him down while we give him insulin."

"Maybe we could get his old diabetes pills down him if we grind them up and mix them with food."

"Okay. Let's give it a try at lunch time."

Bessy made Ken's favorite meal, an omelet with sautéed onions, tomatoes, and bacon bits.

Ken seemed quite cheerful as he entered the kitchen and sat at the table. "Do I smell bacon for lunch?"

Jack said, "Bessy made you an omelet."

"Good. I love omelets." Ken cut a large chunk with his fork. He smiled and chewed for a moment. "What the fuck did you put in this damn thing?" Ken spit out the half-chewed omelet. "You put one of those damn pills in here didn't you? I can taste it." Ken jumped to his feet and pushed the plate off the table. Egg, tomato chunks, bacon, and onions, accompanied by the broken plate, scattered across the tile floor. "I don't need those damn pills. You're trying to poison me."

Ken went to the den and turned on the TV. After flipping through several channels, he settled on re-runs of the Golden Girls. He watched one and a half episodes and then went to his bedroom.

"Let him rest," Bessy said. "The nurse will be here in a little while. When she arrives, the three of us might hold him down and give him some insulin, but now, I should get your bath ready."

Jack went to his bedroom to undress while Bessy went to the bathroom to prepare everything for his bath. With the water adjusted, she called, "Mister Jack. Everything's ready."

Bessy heard no response and went to Jack's room and knocked on the door. She put her ear to the door and heard gasping sounds. "Jack are you alright?" There was no response. She knocked again. *That's strange.* "Jack, I'm coming in."

Bessy opened the door and saw Jack leaning over his bed, hemorrhaging from the mouth. Between bouts of coughing blood, he gasped for air.

"Oh my God," she said.

She helped Jack to a chair and simultaneously took a black towel from the stack beside the bed. She gave it to Jack who held it to his face. While his eyes were covered, Bessy pulled the bloody sheets from his bed, balled them up then threw them out the door. *I don't want him seeing that.*

"Rest a minute," Bessy said calmly. "I'll get your shot."

Seconds later, she returned with a pre-filled syringe of morphine and injected it into his hip.

Jack moved the towel to arm's length and stared at it. "These are big clots," he mumbled weakly. "To-day is the day."

Bessy patted his hand. "The shot will work soon, and you'll feel better."

She handed him a fresh towel then threw the used one out the door.

Jack coughed up a few more clots and then Breathed more easily. The hemorrhage seemed to have stopped.

"Let's get you to bed," Bessy said. "Your bath can wait."

She quickly placed new sheets on the mattress and helped Jack into bed. "You relax. I'm going to page the nurse. Maybe she can come early."

Seconds later, Bessy returned to Jack's bedside. She noted he seemed short of breath so she placed an oxygen mask over his face and started the oxygen. "Try and relax. I think your shot is helping."

Jack nodded then said, "God. Are you here? Are you with me?"

Bessy shook her head. She sat at his side until he seemed comfortable. She patted his hand and whispered, "You relax. I'm going to straighten up the house. Call if you need me."

From the hall, she looked back at Jack. *Hallelujah. He's asleep.*

In the distance, Jack heard the vacuum cleaner being rolled over the wood floor.

"Must be Bessy," he said, opening and then closing his eyes.

Feeling drowsy from his morphine injection, he turned his head to better hear another sound not readily identified. "What the hell is that?" He got out of bed, and holding onto the wall, he made his way next door to Ken's room.

The door was open. He was shocked to see Ken having a seizure. His feet knocked against the foot of the bed as he shook, twitched, and moaned as if dying.

Despite his shortness of breath and weakness, Jack made his way to Ken's bed and managed to pull his lover's stiff body to a semi-upright position and hugged him. "Ken! Ken! What's happing to you? Ken!" The shaking and twitching continued.

Jack called as loudly as he could. "Bessy! Help! Help!" He caught his breath and again called for help. "Damn that woman. Why does she have to vacuum now?"

Jack dragged himself to the door and yelled, "Bessy!! Come here!"

Jack returned to Ken and hugged him as tightly as he could. Ken's jerking continued. Jack began sobbing and tried to yell for help again but the effort was interrupted by a massive hemorrhage. Jack loosened his grip on Ken as both men fell onto the bed.

Ken continued to twitch for a few seconds but then stopped breathing.

With Jack feeling things getting black, he muttered, "God be with us . . ."

The doorbell rang. Bessy stopped vacuuming and went to the door and peered through its window.

"Ah," Bessy said, opening the door for the nurse. "Come in Margaret."

"How you doing?" Margaret asked.

"I'm fine, thank you."

Margaret placed her medical bag on the floor and removed her coat. "And Ken?"

"It's been a rough morning. Mister Ken's blood sugar has been sky high. He refused insulin and won't take his pills. Mister Jack had some hemorrhaging and bad shortness of breath. I felt I had to give him a shot of morphine."

"Then I'd better see him first, but don't worry. You had permission to give the injection if you thought he needed it."

The women went to Jack's room and found it empty.

"Maybe he's with Ken," Margaret said.

Margaret was first in Ken's room. "Oh Lord. There's blood everywhere," she said, feeling Jack's carotid artery for a pulse. She moved her finger to another location and felt the artery for a few more seconds then shook her head. She felt Ken's carotid artery for a few seconds and then stood. "They're both gone."

"Thank you, Lord," Bessy said, shaking her head. "Mister Ken won't be alone."

The End

Love is friendship that
has caught fire. It is quiet
understanding, mutual
confidence, sharing and
forgiving. It is loyalty
through good and bad
times.   It settles for less
than perfection and makes
allowances for human
weaknesses.

Ann Landers

Love and Money

Love and Money

Mark Wilson was the only child of Scott and Linda Wilson, a middle-class family. Scott and his wife were killed in an auto accident when Mark was four.

Having no other living relatives, Mark was raised in Baltimore's St. John orphanage where resources were limited. He grew up wanting more of everything he had and things he did not have.

His intelligence garnered scholarships that made it possible for him to attend a private Catholic school, an ivy league college, and graduate from Harvard's medical school at the age of twenty-three.

As a six-foot four-inch-tall blond man with azure blue eyes, he was hard to overlook. His early interests in gymnastics and weightlifting had added pounds of muscle to what could have been an unassuming lanky body. Unfortunately, his good looks and recognition for excelling in various undertakings caused him to obsess over money and worldly goods. He yearned to buy luxury cars and expensive clothes. His desires led to behaviors aimed at improving his financial situation.

During his internship, he had celebrated his twenty-fourth birthday and developed an attraction for Mary, the vice president of nursing services in his hospital.

Mary, forty years old and divorced, had started

to dye her graying hair and feared growing old alone. She was attracted to Mark's handsome face and athletic build.

He admired her mature beauty, worldliness, sexual experience and bank account filled with alimony, which she gratefully shared with him.

Mark earned a meager income from his internal medicine residency program, and that caused him great angst. At first, he resented Mary's picking up dinner checks, theater, and concert tickets. She bought him clothes, gold jewelry and paid for their vacations. Over time, his sense of shame regarding his financial limitations shrank, and he grew to expect "rewards" for his attention and sexual favors.

Mary and he had a clandestine relationship until he completed his internal medicine residency after which she proudly escorted him to various social affairs in one of three fancy tuxedos she had purchased for him.

While a resident, Mark was constantly chased by nurses, secretaries and a few female doctors, but his time with Mary provided few occasions for him to pursue other interests.

When he concluded his residency training, he joined a very successful group practice in Baltimore. It was headed by an elderly, father-like internist. The practice consisted of seven doctors and many wealthy patients including several multi-millionaires.

Shortly after Mark began his private practice, Mary convinced him to marry her. At first, he seemed happy in the marriage but soon began to eye and flirt with younger women. Several times, Mary caught Mark flirting with two twenty-year-old women—each from millionaire families, but she ignored each incidence as nothing more than the roaming eye she expected of all men.

Mark's fidelity was never in doubt as far as Mary was concerned until one day, after returning from the beauty parlor, she was shocked and surprised when Mark asked her to ease up on the use of black-hair dye. "Black hair makes your facial wrinkles look too harsh," he said. "Lighten up."

Three years into his practice, Mark was called by Doctor Kelly, the head of Mark's medical group, and asked to see a wealthy patient, Judy, in a local emergency room. She was suffering from asthma and allergies.

Mark traveled to the hospital and reviewed the sixty-six-year old patient's medical record.

"That Judy is a lesbian," an ER nurse informed Mark. "Her lover is with her."

"So?" Mark said.

He entered the curtain-enclosed cubicle where Judy was receiving oxygen. The soft beep of her cardiac monitor contrasted with the nonstop, doctor-paging system that joined the cacophony of background noises.

Twenty-six-year-old Sandy, Judy's lover, attended to the patient's comfort needs.

"Hello, Judy. I'm Doctor Mark Wilson. What seems to be bothering you tonight?"

Sandy looked into Mark's face, smiled and said, "Doctor, Judy has allergies to lots of things … including some medicines. She also has asthma that has been well controlled until today. She took her routine medications and several doses of emergency medicines without much effect. Around 8:00 p.m., her condition worsened, so I brought her here."

"Well, let's have a listen to your chest," Mark said, placing his stethoscope against Judy's scrawny chest. "Take in a few deep breaths with your mouth open."

Judy complied as best she could with a fogged

oxygen mask covering her face.

Mark listened to several areas of her chest. "Good! Good. That's fine. Your lungs sound rather tight. I'm going to order a shot of adrenalin for you. That should give you some relief."

A nurse entered the cubicle to check Judy's blood pressure. Mark left, followed by Sandy who tugged at his sleeve.

"Doctor, is this serious?" Sandy asked. "Judy has a chronic heart condition, and I worry about her all the time."

"Anytime a heart patient requires adrenalin is always a serious matter, but don't worry. She's here where we can keep an eye on her. If she does well, we might be able to send her home this evening."

Sandy's lips parted slightly then opened in a big smile. "Thank you, Doctor Mark. Thank you so much."

A nurse gave Judy an adrenalin injection. Within five minutes, she breathed easier.

"She seems to be doing better," Mark said. "I'll check back in a couple of hours."

Mark called the hospital at 10:00 p.m. and spoke to Judy's nurse and then to Sandy. "Sandy, I'm discharging Judy. I'll stop by her house tomorrow evening to see how she's doing. If she relapses, by all means, bring her back to the hospital as soon as you think she's having difficulties."

The next evening, Mark drove up the long gravel driveway to Judy's mansion. He parked his Jaguar convertible at the front door of the castle-like stone home. The evening air was laden with the scent of Jasmine that grew around the fastidiously manicured grounds.

Mark rang the doorbell and admired the carved wooden door before him.

Seconds later, the door squeaked open, and he was greeted by the butler. "Doctor Mark, I presume. Come this way. Miss Judy is in bed and asked that I escort you to her boudoir as soon as you arrived."

The home's atmosphere was dark and brooding. Light barely escaped various Tiffany light fixtures in the great room, over the stairs, and along hallways. Mark had a shudder as he entered a large bedroom dominated by a renaissance-style canopied bed and several large pieces of carved antique furniture. A rose-colored marble fireplace grounded the far center wall. A single lamp illuminated the space adjacent to Judy's bed. Stale air, mixed with the scent of fresh flowers comingled with the smell of wood ashes, too long ignored, filled the dimly lit room.

This place is like a funeral home, Mark thought.

Judy was propped up on expensive looking lace covered pillows. Smelling of baby powder, she extended her pale, bony hand. "Doctor Mark. Thank you for coming. Sandy will be less worried, knowing you're here."

Sandy, half-hidden in the shadow of a wingback chair, stood up. Her tailored dark pink dress moved like a rose, opening on a summer's day. Its short sleeves revealed well trained, muscular arms that spoke for her state of fitness. "Doctor," she said, "you must talk some sense into Judy. She won't rest. She thinks she's immortal and must first-handedly oversee her estate and everything else that goes on around here."

"I'm glad I was able to come," Mark said, "but first, let's get some more lights on. I like to see my patients."

Mark checked Judy's pulse and blood pressure while Sandy turned on more lights. He untied the blue ribbons that closed Judy's lace-fronted gown then listened intently to her lungs.

"Your lungs sound much better tonight. Your

heart is a little irregular but nothing to worry about . . . given your history." He folded his stethoscope and placed it in his bag. "Young lady, I suggest you take a break from unimportant things. Rest as much as you can . . . at least for the next several days.

Tying her gown closures, Judy said, "Doctor, I'm an old lady devoted to enjoying as much of life as I can . . . for as long as I can. Can you stay a few minutes and have a drink with me . . . and Sandy too? It's my bedtime relaxant. We hate to drink alone."

Mark contemplated his options.

"Well . . . maybe a small glass of sherry," Mark said with a tone of capitulation in his voice.

Sandy summoned the butler. He arrived carrying a silver tray containing glasses and a crystal decanter of sherry, Judy's favorite bedtime drink. The butler poured the sherry. Sandy handed a glass to Judy and then to Mark.

As the glass passed to Mark, Sandy deliberately rubbed her hand and expensively manicured nails against the inside of his hand. She looked him in the eye and smiled.

Mark smiled back, a rush of adrenalin flooding over him. He knew he was being wooed by this curvaceous, spitfire-of-a-woman with a gym-worked body.

The trio finished their sherry over small talk.

Mark looked at the tall clock in the corner. "Oh, my. Look at the time. I'm sorry to say I must be on my way."

"I'll see you to the door," Sandy said as Mark rose to leave.

"How nice of you." Turning toward Judy, he said, "Make sure you rest. I'll look in on you tomorrow evening . . . see how you're doing."

Sandy escorted Mark to the door and gave him a tight hug. Her embrace lasted longer than custom allowed, but Mark enjoyed the intimacy. Her breasts felt firm against his chest. *She's had implants,* Mark thought. He tightened his embrace, letting his hands move slowly down the back of her soft wool dress. He inhaled deeply. She smelled of expensive perfume.

Sandy kissed Mark on the cheek, released her embrace, and opened the door.

"See you tomorrow," she said then smiled.

"Tomorrow," Mark replied, his hand sliding down Sandy's bare arm.

The next day, Mark arrived at Judy's house at 7:00 p.m. This time, he was greeted at the door by Sandy. She wore a red, tight-fitting, see-through dress with a deeply plunging neck line. She gave Mark a tight hug and raised her knee to his crotch.

For a moment, Mark pushed his crotch against her knee and grabbed her ass with each hand. "We had better get upstairs," he said, "Remember I'm here to see Judy."

In Judy's bedroom, Mark took his stethoscope from his bag then listened to Judy's lungs and heart. "All seems to be pretty good tonight. Your lungs have cleared."

"Well then, that calls for some sherry," Judy said, pulling a fancy butler tassel.

Moments later, the butler arrived with sherry.

Mark pulled his chair beside Judy's bed, so he could feel her pulse. Sandy handed him a glass of sherry and pulled her chair close to his.

"Here's a toast to better days," Mark said.

"To better days," Judy and Sandy said.

Sandy's foot slid stealthily over the antique silk carpet until it touched Mark's shoe. She tapped it lightly.

Mark moved his ankle behind Sandy's ankle and gently moved it up and down her leg. Sandy smiled as she looked at her sherry. The two shared several foot and ankle nudges as they drank.

Finally, Mark had to take his leave. He was escorted to the door by Sandy who repeated her intimate hug, but this time, her hand found its way to Mark's crotch. Sandy quickly discerned that Mark was interested in her attention. He left excited to know that he would be seeing Sandy again.

Mark and Sandy met secretly on several occasions in various venues. Each person seemed infatuated with the other, and each wanted more and more of the other's time.

Several months passed and Sandy began announcing her love for Mark. He repeatedly said he wanted to spend more time with her, but he feared Mary would discover their extramarital affair and divorce him. He didn't have a prenuptial agreement, so divorce would ruin him financially.

"Well, I know a way out…if you're up for it," Sandy said, "but it will only work with the aid of your medical expertise."

"What are you getting at?" Mark asked.

"I know Judy has willed her entire estate to me. She was never married, has no children or known living relatives, but she does have serious allergies. Hell, you already know that, *Doctor*. Some evening, when you're at the house, we could expose Judy to one of the things she's allergic to. That would cause a serious allergic reaction requiring serious medicine. You would give adrenalin to supposedly treat the attack except . . . you'd give a little more adrenalin than required."

Marks eyelids were so wide with disbelief his

eyes felt they were on the verge of falling out of their sockets.

"I've heard that adrenalin can cause a fatal heart attack." Sandy said. "No one would be suspicious if Judy died of a heart attack, and . . . I'd become a multi-millionaire. I'd have enough money for both of us—for life. Then, you could divorce Mary without fear of being broke."

"My god, Sandy! Do you know what you're saying—no, *asking* of me?"

"Yes, but do you know what it would mean for both of us? You think about it. Money. Freedom."

A week later, Mark and Sandy were having another of their clandestine meetings. They had the hottest sex since they began seeing each other. They lay on the sweat-soaked sheets, exhausted and quietly looking at each other.

Mark broke the silence after he and Sandy had recovered.

"Sandy, I've been thinking about what you suggested last week. I'd be willing to participate—provided you spilt the estate fifty-fifty." He was quiet for a moment. "Is it a deal?"

After a few seconds of pensiveness, Sandy said, "It's a deal."

"What are we going to do about the butler?" Mark asked.

"Don't worry about him," Sandy said, "He's never around unless he's called. We'll let your adrenalin work its 'magic' until we're certain of the outcome. Then we call the butler and 911."

"Maybe we should call the butler as soon as she starts having symptoms of the allergic reaction. Let him see me ask you and her about the use of adrenalin . . .

explain the dangers, and then you say 'go ahead,' but you have to look worried. Understand? *Damn worried*."

"Believe me, I understand."

Mark continued, "We only need a few minutes of heart stoppage for the brain and heart to be irreversibly damaged. I'll kill a few minutes listening to her heart, checking her pulse, and listening to her lungs. Then we ask the butler to call 911 while I start CPR. The butler and the EMTs must see us doing CPR."

There were a few moments of silence.

"You know we could go to jail for life if it's determined we intentionally created the outcome," Mark said.

"Yes, but we won't get caught. We have to remember to throw things around the room to make everyone think we were acting in haste."

"We should drag Judy onto the floor, so we can say we needed a firmer surface than the mattress to do the CPR."

"Sound good. I'd buy it," Sandy said, smiling.

Mark quietly stared at Sandy for a moment. "I want to get this over with quickly. You need to start exposing Judy to increasing amounts of something *you* know she's allergic to. I don't want to know what that is, but after she starts showing signs of wheezing, have the butler phone my service and request a house-call. Make sure the butler knows she's wheezing. That's critical."

Three evenings later the deed was done. The coroner interviewed Mark's answering service personnel, the EMTs, the butler, Sandy and Mark.

Judy's post mortem blood tests revealed an above normal level of adrenalin, but it was consistent with an emergency attempt to save her life. The coroner signed the death certificate and wrote, "Death due to natural causes. Heart failure."

Following Judy's death, Mark and Sandy decided to remain apart for a few weeks.

In the past, Sandy had seen another physician in Mark's medical group for her personal healthcare. Acting on her doctor's suggestion, Sandy phoned his office and asked for an appointment for treatment of depression, secondary to Judy's demise. Sandy's doctor wasn't available, so she was assigned to see Mark.

At first Mark did not want to see her but acquiesced to Sandy's request. This arrangement provided cover for some intimate meetings. Behind the closed examination room door, they engaged in everything except intercourse. The prolonged time they spent together in the office was attributed to counseling for Sandy's depression following Judy's death. To bolster the alibi, Mark prescribed an antidepressant. Sandy filled the prescription but never took the pills.

Four months after Judy's death, her will was probated. Sandy was awarded the house, cars, furniture, art and fifty-three million dollars in stocks, bonds and cash. Much to everyone's surprise, Judy left Mark $1,000,000.00 for his "faithful service" as her private physician. With Judy's cash in hand, Sandy and Mark had clandestine meetings out of town.

Mark's excuse to Mary for being away was usually attributed to medical conferences and educational courses.

Sandy cautioned Mark not to be impatient about receiving his half of her inherited assets. "We don't want to be seen spending too much money too soon," she advised, "and I can't hand out 25 million dollars willy nilly either. Bankers, brokers and attorneys would suspect something if all that money went out in a lump sum to one person . . . especially the man who was present when Judy died."

"You make sense, but I so want that Bentley convertible I've seen."

"I understand," Judy said, "but I know you're also interested in that penthouse condo with the huge terrace on 5th Avenue. How about I buy it and let you use it until I can begin distributing the assets in a safe way?"

"Needless to say, I'd like to have my money as soon as possible, but I agree we have to be careful. You buy the condo but pay the maintenance fees and taxes five years in advance. We can also shop for furniture, but you'll have to pay the bills, Sandy. My tastes are expensive, and *I* can't afford to buy what I want . . . not without my half of the estate."

Four weeks later, Sandy closed on the penthouse condo.

One of their out-of-town rendezvouses occurred in New York City where Mark was allegedly attending a medical conference. While there, they shopped for condo furnishings that met his expensive taste.

One pleasant afternoon as Mark and Sandy walked along New York's 5th Avenue, they passed Tiffany's jewelry store. They paused and did some window shopping.

Mark noted one diamond ring that sparkled more than any other ring in the small window. "Look at that ring! I think I should buy it for Mary. I'm afraid she's going to suspect something bad about our marriage if I keep traveling without asking her to tag along."

"Sounds like a good idea, but haven't you

already bought her something with the money Judy left you?" Sandy asked.

"Oh, I'm not going to use *my* money for gifts. That's being saved for building my own medical center." Without batting an eye, Mark said, "I was hoping you would buy the ring . . . for me. I mean for me for Mary."

Sandy stood stiffly erect, rolled her shoulders backwards, and took a deep breath. "God, you have balls!" With words squeezed through tight lips, she said, "Let's see how much it costs."

They entered the brightly lighted store. Noting classical music playing in the background, they casually explored several glass cases displaying rings with large diamonds.

A pretentious acting salesman, wearing too much Polo cologne, approached them. "Welcome to Tiffany's. May I help you?"

"We'd like to have a closer look at one of the diamond rings in your window," Mark said. "It's the diamond solitaire in the middle row, last one on the left."

Within minutes, the salesman had retrieved the ring and invited the couple to sit on silk covered Louis XV chairs at a counter. The salesman placed the ring on a burgundy velvet pad. His carefully manicured fingers pushed the pad toward Sandy. Smiling, he said, "Do have a look."

"Oh it's lovely," Sandy said, holding the ring to the light. "It certainly does sparkle. How many carats?"

The salesman looked at the white tag hanging from the ring. "It weighs 5.4 carats. It's GIA certified as to cut, clarity, etc. It's a beautiful stone. Do you like the setting?"

"The whole package is beautiful," Sandy said, handing the ring to Mark.

"I agree," Mark said. "How much is it?"

The salesman looked at the codes on the ring's tag. "It's only $189,000."

"Wow!" Mark said. "It's beautiful. I think we should take it."

Sandy looked at Mark, frowned, and nudged his leg with her knee. There was an awkward moment of silence. Finally, Sandy quietly said, "Do you really think we should spend that much money on a ring?"

"It's worth it," Mark said, "She will love it."

"Oh, you're buying it for someone else?" the salesman asked.

"Yes, we're buying it for . . . our mother," Mark answered, nudging Sandy's foot as he spoke.

"Okay. We'll take it," Sandy said, handing the salesman a credit card.

Gift-wrapped ring in hand, the couple left the store.

For two more days, they took in city sites buying furniture for Mark's penthouse, seeing Broadway shows, and enjoying the city's better restaurants before returning to Baltimore.

A few minutes after Mark returned home, he presented the ring to Mary. She was ecstatic. She hugged and kissed him repeatedly, removed the original, smaller engagement ring from her finger and replaced it with the new diamond. It sparkled as she waved her hand in the air with the glee of a teenager.

"You shouldn't have," Mary said, "I know you inherited a million dollars, but I thought it was being saved for your building."

"Don't you worry, honey. You're worth it. I just hope you like it."

"Like it. I love it!"

Several days later, Mary prepared to visit an up-scale jewelry store in search of a set of shirt studs and cuff links. They were to be a gift for Mark who had hinted he wanted something different for his new tuxedo shirt.

Mary dressed as if she was going to a luncheon at the White House. Her ensemble included the only haute couture suit she owned. It consisted of a navy-blue serge skirt and waist length jacket hand sewn by Valentino Garavani. Under the jacket she wore a rich-looking, cream-colored, silk blouse. Over it, she layered several silver necklaces and one containing antique amber. She chose a dark blue straw hat with a cream-colored satin ribbon around its crown.

She latched on her gold dinner watch and smiled as she pushed her new diamond ring onto her finger. Standing tall and proud before her mirror, she adjusted her hat and examined her image with a large measure of coyness. She was ready to shop.

After perusing several jewelry cases in the up-scale shop, she found one case with several sets of shirt studs and matching cuff links. Examining one particular set up close, her haughty-acting salesman noticed her large, flashy ring.

"Now that's a very nice diamond," he said. "May I have a closer look at it?"

"Surely," Mary replied, removing the ring.

The jeweler pulled out his loop, pushed it onto his baggy eyelids, and examined the diamond in detail.

"Ah ha . . . Someone likes you *very* much," he said.

"Well . . . he does. I'm curious. How much is this ring worth?"

"In our shop . . . we would sell this ring for . . . $200,000. I noticed it's signed *Tiffany,* so it possibly sold for more than $200,000 in Tiffany's store."

"Wow! I had no idea," Mary said, flashing a large grin. "I'm really here to buy that set of 18k gold tuxedo studs and cuff links for my husband."

"Very well. I'll wrap them for you," the jeweler said, taking her credit card.

Mary left the store clutching her husband's gift. She thought. *I can't believe Mark spent $200,000 on a ring. And for me!*

Mary continued to window shop at various stores. Along the way, she passed an ATM machine. Curiosity got the better of her. She opened her purse and withdrew the silver cardholder that contained her bank card. She placed the card in the machine, entered her PIN, and selected the screen number for Mark's building account. She noted there had been no withdrawals since the account was opened. *Maybe he used his credit card*
to buy the ring. I'll watch for the monthly statement.

Mark's and Mary's life went on as usual until the day the credit card bill arrived. Normally, Mark handled the financial matters, but Mary was too curious to ignore the latest statement.

If I open this, will he suspect something? Maybe I should look at the bill after Mark has opened it. I know where they're kept after the checks are written. Hmmm. What to do? What to do?

Mary placed the unopened statement on Mark's desk and walked away. Five minutes later, she returned and took the envelope to the kitchen. After a few minutes of steaming it, the flap opened. Mary examined the bill. *There are no charges from Tiffany's. How the hell did he pay for this ring?*

She allowed the envelope to dry; then replaced

the bill and glued the flap shut.

How the hell did he get the money to pay for the ring? Did he borrow the money? From whom? Did he steal it? From his partners? Oh god! I hope not. Besides, who has that kind of cash lying around? Did he win it at gambling? I've never known him to gamble. Did he beg it? Mark doesn't beg. Well, not real begging. He expects. Did someone give him the money? Who would give him that much money? Oh my god! Some woman must have given him money . . . a wealthy woman. But why? "Oh my god! Oh my god! I don't want to believe it … No. I don't. I don't!" She took a deep breath and let it out slowly. *Calm down, Mary. Calm down, girl. Lately, he has been gone a lot but for educational things.*

Mary tried to remain her normal self when Mark arrived home that night. They exchanged a light kiss and Mark sat at the kitchen table to eat a left-over-dinner.

"How was your day?" he asked.

"Nothing unusual," Mary replied in a shaky voice.

"Any interesting mail or phone calls?" Mark asked, looking up from his plate.

Mary swallowed hard. "Just some bills. They're on your desk."

Mark ate dinner and then reviewed the mail. Later, he and Mary watched some favorite TV programs then went to bed. Mark immediately fell asleep.

Mary stared at the ceiling for hours. She pulled the cool sheets to her chin and tried to think soothing thoughts, but she couldn't stop the mental questions she had about "another woman." At 2:00 a.m., she went to the medicine chest, found her rarely used sleeping pills, and washed down one large capsule with a glass of water. She returned to bed and in a short time, fell asleep.

The next morning, Mark left the house at 8:00 a.m.

Mary immediately reviewed the credit card statement again. There was no billing for the ring.

Mary decided she had to follow Mark for a few days to put to rest the troubling questions she had about their relationship and the possibility of Mark seeing another woman.

At 9:00 a.m., she phoned Mark's office. When he finally came to the phone, she asked an inane question but was relieved to know he was working in his office.

Mark normally makes hospital rounds at 11:00 a.m., has lunch in the doctor's cafeteria in the hospital at noon, completes paperwork in the medical records department, and then returns to his office around 2:00 p.m. He doesn't have time to see anyone in the middle of the day.

Nevertheless, Mary decided to rent a car to reduce the possibility of her being discovered, and drove by the doctor's parking lot at the hospital. She wanted to see if his car was there.

Mary arrived at noon and saw his car parked near the doctor's entrance to the hospital. She drove a short distance from the lot and parked in the shadow of a large maple tree. She didn't want to be seen when Mark exited the lot.

She waited for what seemed like days. She twisted her hair and bit her nails then resorted to relaxation techniques and chair yoga as she waited.

At 2:15 p.m., Mark left the lot and drove toward his office. Mary, lagging behind, passed the office and parked six hundred feet down the block, watching Mark park in the office lot. She listened to the radio and scanned magazines with an occasional glance in her rearview mirror at Mark's car. It hadn't moved in two hours.

At 4:30 p.m., Mark entered his car and drove away from Mary's position. He took the road leading to their home. Mary turned her car around and rushed to catch up with Mark's Jaguar. She followed him, from a discrete distance, for fifteen minutes. Instead of turning on to the street leading home, he continued straight ahead.

Where the hell is he going?

Mark pulled into the underground parking lot of a luxury, high rise condominium. *Why the hell is he going in there?* Mary stopped her car at the top of the entrance ramp. *Now what do I do?*

The building's garage gate was still open. Mary gunned her car down its ramp and into the garage. Once past the gate, she slammed on the brakes. She looked around but didn't see Marks' car. She parked close to the garage entrance in case she had to make a hasty get away.

Her heart beating with the rapidity of a firing machine gun, she walked toward the elevator and watched the elevator's floor-indicator. The elevator had stopped at the PH level.

He's going to a penthouse. It takes money to own a penthouse apartment in this part of town. I've heard a lot of wealthy widows live in this building. So far this fits my suspicions. Now, how do I get up there? I need a key to call the elevator.

Mary glanced at the elevator's floor-indicator. The elevator was coming down. She moved away from the elevator door and backed into a small space out of sight of the elevator.

Moments later, the elevator opened, and an elderly couple exited the cabin then walked away from Mary's location. She dashed toward the open door and managed to enter the elevator just as the door started to close. Its rubber safety bumper barely touched her.

"Whew! That was close."

Mary pushed the penthouse button and stepped to the rear of the elevator. The elevator's thick carpet absorbed Mary's light weight with luxurious ease. The spacious, wood-paneled cabin was filled with an overspray of air freshener. At the 5th floor, the elevator stopped with a slight bounce causing its light fixture crystals to tinkle. The door opened, and an older man, with glistening-white hair, and a dark tan entered.

"Afternoon," he said.

"Afternoon," Mary replied as the door closed.

After a moment of silence, Mary said, "Sir, do you live in this building?"

"Yes, I do," he said, looking at the only illuminated button on the floor selector panel. "I live on the floor below your destination."

The man pushed the button for his floor.

"Do you know Doctor Mark Wilson?" Mary asked.

"Yes. He lives on the penthouse level."

"I'm on my way to his apartment, and I've forgotten the apartment number the receptionist gave me."

"Yes. I know him. He lives in PH 2, right over my apartment."

"Thank you very much. I'd forget my head if it wasn't hooked on," Mary said, smiling.

"No problem. Well, this is my floor. Have a good afternoon," the man said, leaving the elevator.

"Thanks for your help."

On the penthouse level, Mary crept through the plush surroundings to apartment PH 2. She stood quietly listening at the door. She heard nothing.

Maybe he's not here. Oh, god! I've got to find out what's going on.

Mary pushed the doorbell and waited as the Westminster Chimes rang deep inside the apartment.

"I'm coming. I'm coming," someone said from within.

The door opened, and Mary gasped

With a questioning look on her face, a woman dressed in a thin, flowing silk robe stared at Mary.

"I thought you were a delivery person," the woman said, tying the belt to her sheer dressing robe. "May I help you?"

"I'm sorry. I must have the wrong apart—"

"Who is it honey?" a male voice yelled from a distant room.

Bare chested, Mark walked into view. "Oh my god!" he said. "Mary. What are you doing here?"

"I should be asking you that question!" Mary yelled.

"For god's sake don't just stand there yelling in the hall," the woman said, "Come in and close the door. Let's be civil."

"Civil! You expect *me* to be civil when I'm confronted with my husband's mistress in their den of iniquity?" Mary spoke with staccato speech, shifting her hips and shaking her finger. "Lady, I'm mad as hell, and I'm *not* shutting up!"

"Quiet down!" Mark yelled. "Quiet down. I can explain everything. It's not what you think."

Shaking her fist, Mary asked, "How the hell do you know what I'm thinking? You son-of-a bitch. You home wrecker!"

"I can see you're upset, but calm down," Mark said, standing stiffly erect, patting the air.

"Upset! I'm mad as hell you god damn gigolo," Mary yelled, her face growing hotter.

"Settle down for god's sake, Mark said, "We're

adults. Act like one."

"How do you expect me to quiet down when I know I've been *lied* to, *cheated* on and god only knows what else?" Mary turned toward the woman. "By the way, *honey*, I think I've seen your picture in the papers. Aren't you Sandy somebody? The one who recently inherited millions of dollars from Mark's former patient. You're *the* new multi-millionairess?"

"Really," Sandy said, "Who knows what you can read in the papers?"

"I was wondering where Mark had gotten the money for this ring," Mary said, thrusting her ring-bearing hand under Sandy's nose, "Now I know—you!"

There was a pregnant pause as Mary had unsettling thoughts. "Oh my god! What else have I uncovered?" *Mark has supposedly been to lots of out of town medical meetings, but he's been seeing this bitch. This bitch with lots of money, money she inherited from the dead woman that Mark took care of. The newspapers said the rich woman died unexpectedly with Mark and this bitch at her side. Did he, could he, do her in? Oh God. He did. I know he did.*

Mary stared Mark in the eye. "You helped this bitch kill that rich woman for her money, didn't you? *Didn't you?*"

"You're just an upset, jilted wife," Mark said, walking onto the terrace with a glass of scotch he picked up from a side table.

"Don't you dare walk away from *me*!" Mary yelled, her voice rising. "I'm not through with you!"

"Let's face it, Mary. I have expensive taste. *You* can't afford me on your nurse's salary. You and I know there's only one course of action now. Divorce. Get out of here, call your attorney. Let's get this over with!"

Sandy followed Mark and Mary onto the terrace.

"For god's sake quiet down, Mary," Sandy said. "You'll be heard all over town."

Mary shoved Sandy back into the apartment and continued her tirade. "Mark, you've never been interested in *anything* but money. Now, you have a rich girlfriend. Did you help her get the money? Did you? Did you *deliver* the money to *this* woman? Did you, Mark? Do you have blood on your hands?"

"Mary, I don't know what you're talking about. Now get out of here. Go home."

"Well, don't bother coming home *mister greedy*. I'm having the locks changed. And as for this ring—"

Sandy, interrupting Mary who held the diamond ring in her palm, said, "Mark thought you deserved the ring. Keep it."

"Somehow I don't think Mark wanted me to have this ring," Mary said, "To him it's money. Just money. That's the only thing that interests him. I don't want this damn ring or his money, or should I say *your* money!"

Mary tossed the ring at Mark standing by the terrace railing.

Sandy must have believed the ring would fall over the railing and bolted to catch it.

Mark stretched his right arm toward the ring arcing high over the terrace and beyond the railing. He managed to grasp it, but onrushing Sandy slammed into him. Both lost their footing and fell over the railing. They plummeted, screaming, toward the cobblestone driveway below. Mark's hand gripped the ring as he fell.

Two thuds, in rapid succession, rose from below, and then all was quiet

Mary forced herself to the edge of the terrace and peered over the railing at the carnage twenty-four floors below. She slumped to the terrace, head in her hands, as a flood of emotions released a torrent of tears. She wept uncontrollably.

She soon heard excited voices from below and then sirens in the distance. The sound of the sirens drew closer and finally stopped below the terrace.

Within minutes the condo's doorman and police entered Mark's apartment. The officers approached Mary with guns drawn.

"Put your hands up!" a policeman shouted, "Put your hands up!"

Mary complied. "I have no weapons."

A policewoman searched the apartment for possible accomplices.

"Get up!" the policeman ordered, "Step inside the apartment."

Mary, still crying, walked into the apartment and sat on a sofa. The officers calmly questioned her as to what had happened. The policewoman offered her a handkerchief.

Mary told her story broken by long periods of crying and sobbing.

An hour later, Mary had regained her composure and was escorted toward a patrol car. In the lobby, she noted detectives interviewing the doorman and several condo owners who had been near the main door at the time of the couple's fall.

Mary and her police escorts crossed the driveway, passing pools of blood and the sheet-covered bodies of Mark and Sandy. Mary paused and stared at the sheets. "Mark, why did you do this to me? Why? Why?"

Onlookers spoke in hushed tones and pointed toward Mary as though she was a murderer.

At police headquarters, Mary was interviewed by homicide detectives. During the interview, the detectives were interrupted by another detective who called them out of the room.

"Joe," the interrupting detective said to one of the interviewing detectives, "The ring was still in the dead man's hand. When he grabbed it, he must have unintentionally put the tip of his ring finger through the ring's loop. It wasn't dislodged by the fall. The part of her story about a ring checks out."

The detectives were quiet for a few seconds then one said, "Let's take this to the boss. I'm inclined to let Mary go."

The supervisor was phoned and listened to the details of the case. She rendered a decision and the detective hung up the phone. The detectives returned to the interview room where Mary waited.

"Mary, we've discussed the case with our supervisor. We've reached a decision. We see no reason to detain you any longer. The prosecutor will review your case, but for now, you're free to go. A grand jury may or may not hear your case, but we believe what happened was a . . . horrible accident."

"Thank you, Detective. May I have a ride home?"

Turning to a staff sergeant, the detective said, "Please drive Mrs. Wilson home."

"Oh, Mrs. Wilson, we'll probably return the ring after the prosecutor reviews the case."

"Thanks, but no thanks. Send it anonymously to the Saint John orphanage."

The End

To feel much for others and little for ourselves; to restrain our selfishness and exercise our benevolent affections constitute the perfection of human nature.

Adam Smith

Brad Barham has written two other gay-themed novels: *A Façade of Muscles* and *Hiding From the Blind.*

www.ingramcontent.com/pod-product-compliance
Lightning Source LLC
Chambersburg PA
CBHW061752020426
42331CB00006B/1444